Ian Carroll is a best selling author, with a paperback and also on Kindle.

Ian is the author of the 'A-Z of Bloody titles – *'Warning: Water May Contain Aisle 3'* and *'Pensioner'*. Also the aut Ishmael', 'Demon Pirates Vs. Vikings – Blackhorns ... *Guide to Internet Dating'* and *'Valentines Day'*.

'Hammer Horror' is also the first book in *'The Movie Fans Have Their Say'* series of Books, with many more planned for the future.

He is also the author of the music books –
'Lemmy: Memories of a Rock 'N' Roll Legend' – which was a #1 in the UK, USA, Canada, France and Germany – *'Ronnie James Dio: Man on the Silver Mountain – Memories of a Rock 'N' Roll Icon'*, *'Leonard Cohen: Just One More Hallelujah'*, *'Music, Mud and Mayhem: The Official History of the Reading Festival'* and *'From Donington to Download: The History of Rock at Donington Park'*.

The First eight Volumes of the *'Fans Have Their Say...'* series are also available which are:

'The Fans Have Their Say #1 KISS - We Wanted the Best and We Got the Best'.
'The Fans Have Their Say #2 AC/DC – Rock 'N' Roll From the Land Down Under'.
'The Fans Have Their Say #3 BLACK SABBATH – The Lords of Darkness'.
'The Fans Have Their Say #4 GUNS 'N ROSES – Welcome to the Jungle...'
'The Fans Have Their Say #5 METALLICA – Exit, Light, Enter, Night'
'The Fans Have Their Say #6 QUEEN – Is This the Real Life...?'
'The Fans Have Their Say #7 ELTON JOHN – Count the Headlights on the Highway...'
'The Fans Have Their Say #8 MEAT LOAF – All Revved Up...'
'The Fans Have Their Say #9 DEF LEPPARD – Steel-City Rock Stars

Ian has also written the history section for the Official Reading Festival music site in the UK and has attended the festival 32 times since 1983.

Ian lives with his wife Raine, two sons – Nathan & Josh plus Stanley and the memories of a jet-black witches cat called Rex - in Plymouth, Devon, UK.

www.iancarrollauthor.com
Facebook.com/iancarrollauthor (Various Book Pages as well)
ian@iancarrollauthor.com

© Ian Carroll 2019

ISBN- *9781689931557*

The Fans Have Their Say #10

Bon Jovi

New Jersey's Finest

© Ian Carroll 2019

My Introduction to Bon Jovi

When I was growing up I initially came across Bon Jovi by pure accident. I had heard the name but managed to see them for the first time at the Cornwall Coliseum, which used to be in St. Austell in Cornwall, UK. Below is a short piece from one of my previous Books '***Welcome to Cornwall Coliseum***'.

"One of my favourite bands of all time, for KISS to play so near to where I lived was unbelievable when they headlined the Coliseum on the

'Animalize' tour. With their 'brand new' guitarist Bruce Kulick having just joined to replace the ill Mark St. John.

The support band was a new band that I had heard of on the 'Friday Rock Show', a little band from New Jersey called Bon Jovi.

Jon Bon Jovi, complete with a string vest and the curliest of shaggy perms, lead his band through tracks from the first album that was yet to be released, they went down well, but not as well as KISS.

Performing all the classics and some tracks from the new 'Animalize' album, KISS were still in their 'without make-up' stage and so were 'glammed up' with their clothes instead.

A brilliant night of American rock 'n' roll and the only time that KISS has ever played in Cornwall."

Ian Carroll (Author)

Bon Jovi @ Cornwall Coliseum
St. Austell, UK
October 2nd 1984

Break Out
Come Back
Roulette
Shot Through The Heart
Get Ready
Runaway

And that was my first experience of seeing the Legends that would become of the biggest and best, good time rock 'n' roll bands in the world, all the way from New Jersey to a venue that sadly is no more, less than an hour from my home.

The next time I got to see them was at Donington Park Monsters of Rock Festival a year later in 1985.

I went to the Festival on my own, but made friends with a young lady there with similar tastes and we relished in seeing Bon Jovi playing tracks from their latest album '**7800° Fahrenheit**' – having already watched Ratt and Magnum – who I absolutely loved as well. Also on the bill were the relatively unknown (but known to me) Metallica – who were promoting their 'Ride the Lightning' album.

The post in my book '***From Donington to Download***' is as follows and pretty much covers Bon Jovi's performance.

*"Bon Jovi were making their debut at Donington, only to return 2 years later as triumphant headliners. Their album '**7800° Fahrenheit**' had been released four months before and so was already a favourite with their adoring fans; tracks included from it on the day featured were '**Only Lonely**', '**In And Out Of Love**' and the rousing '**Tokyo Road**' as their opener."*

Monsters of Rock Festival, Donington Park, UK, 17th August 1985

Tokyo Road
Breakout
Only Lonely
Runaway
In and Out of Love
I Don't Want to Go Home
Get Ready

As seemed to be the habit, I was lucky enough to see Bon Jovi the following year – this time in London – so that was three years in a row. The show this time was on a cold winters evening in November at the legendary London music venue, the Hammersmith Odeon - as it was called then and as it will always be to me and countless other music fans the country over.

The support this evening was Queensryche – who I was very keen to catch for the second time – but due to my girlfriend at the time (Mandy) and her friend Julia dithering in the local Wimpy, we turned up to see them say goodbye and leave the stage! To say that I was annoyed was a complete understatement, I was seething, but the annoyance would dissipate as Bon Jovi hit the stage.

Playing seven songs from their new LP '**Slippery When Wet**' they were on fire. We were seeing a band that were rocketing to stardom and they had the tunes, the personalities and the sometimes elusive 'likeability factor'. Women loved Bon Jovi and men wanted to be them, so the Hammersmith Odeon was filled with leopard print, fringed leathers and cowboy boots – myself included, it just had to be done.

The show at Hammersmith was amazing and with T-shirt purchased, we all had the feeling that we had just witnessed a band that would be playing bigger and better shows as their record back catalogue grew. Little did we know that they would be back at Donington a year later to headline Monsters of Rock and I would be seeing them for the fourth time in four separate years!

Hammersmith Odeon
London, UK,
24th November 1986

Pink Flamingoes
Raise Your Hands
Breakout
Tokyo Road
You Give Love a Bad Name
Wild in the Streets
Silent Night
Livin' on a Prayer
Let It Rock
In and Out of Love
Runaway
Wanted Dead or Alive
The Boys Are Back in Town
Drift Away

Back at Monsters of Rock the following year at Donington – the Home of Rock – Bon Jovi topped a bill that was, for the first time, all American bands and quality bands as well. The following entry is once again from my book '***From Donington to Download***' and it fully captures the event.

"Bon Jovi at the time in '87 were riding high on the success of the ***'Slippery When Wet'*** *album and Donington at the time was probably one of their biggest shows; nine of the ten tracks on the album were played on the day, with a selection from the previous two albums.*
For the final encore of 'We're An American Band' by Grand Funk Railroad, Bon Jovi were joined onstage by Paul Stanley (KISS), Dee Snider (Twisted Sister) and Bruce Dickinson (Iron Maiden); Bruce let the 'cat out of the bag' that he would be back to headline with Iron Maiden the following year and KISS would make their debut the following year as well.
Jon Bon Jovi was wearing a beard at Donington for this performance and looked very unlike his usual clean cut, boy next door, rock star image."

Jon Bon Jovi – complete with Beard – at Donington '87

Richie Sambora in the spotlight at Donington '87

Monsters of Rock Festival
Donington Park, UK
22nd August 1987

Pink Flamingoes
Raise Your Hands
I'd Die for You
Tokyo Road
You Give Love a Bad Name
Wild in the Streets
Not Fade Away
Never Say Goodbye
Livin' on a Prayer
Let It Rock
Get Ready
Runaway
Wanted Dead or Alive
Drift Away
Travelin' Band
We're an American Band

Sadly the last time I saw Bon Jovi was at their triumphant headline slot at the Milton Keynes Bowl in 1989 – I was booked up to see them at the Etihad in Manchester in 2013, but circumstances changed and I wasn't able to go. I actually went to Dartmouth to see my new girlfriend, now my wife, so things turned out all right in the end.

The show at the Milton Keynes Bowl was their first of 8, from 1989 - '06, covering many tours and double nights.

The Milton Keynes Bowl, prior to the Skid Row set

The day was just the perfect rock line up featuring 3 bands that were quite large for support. The supporting cast on the day was Skid Row, Vixen and Europe and the crowd was as expected – MASSIVE and it was a blisteringly hot day as well.

The tour was in support of the '*New Jersey*' album and was called '*New Jersey Syndicate*' – the full UK tour would come in December of this year, with the Bowl being the only summer date – apart from an appearance at Tower Records, Piccadilly Circus in London where '*Ride Cowboy Ride*' and '*Wanted Dead or Alive*' were performed, two days prior to this outdoor festival date.

The set ended with an amazing cover of 'Walk This Way' with both Steven Tyler and Joe Perry from Aerosmith joining the boys on stage.

Milton Keynes National Bowl
'New Jersey Syndicate' Tour
19th August 1989

Lay Your Hands on Me
I'd Die For You
Wild in the Streets
You Give Love a Bad Name
Pink Flamingos
Let It Rock
Living in Sin
Blood on Blood
Runaway
Livin' on a Prayer
Wanted Dead or Alive
The Boys Are Back in Town
Walk This Way
Bad Medicine
Shout

So that was my introduction to Bon Jovi, one of the greatest rock 'n' roll bands on the planet – always were, still are. Still filling stadiums from Sydney to San Francisco, from Madrid to Manchester – full of fans that mostly watch them on every tour – never missing show, when the Bon Jovi train ploughs into their hometown.

I spoke to some fans who have seen them over 50 times – this is much more difficult in the UK with their latest tour being the first one in 6 years – last in the UK in 2013.

This book goes out to the lucky fans who have seen them tour all across America over the years and the fans in the smaller countries like the UK, where to see them perform is more of a treat, due to the large gaps between appearances – I'm not jealous, I'm just saying.

So, hope you all enjoy reading this book with the accounts of fans from all over the world – the 10th Book in this series, why not check out the others? – and have fun reading the reviews of the albums and looking at some great photos.

Take care and remember '*Let It Rock*'.

Ian Carroll
(August 2019)

Bon Jovi

1) Runaway.........................3:50
2) Roulette.........................4:38
3) She Don't Know Me..............3:58
4) Shot Through the Heart.........4:16
5) Love Lies.......................4:06
6) Breakout........................5:20
7) Burning for Love...............3:51
8) Come Back.......................3:56
9) Get Ready.......................4:07

Release Date: 21ˢᵗ January 1984
Producer: **Tony Bongiovi / Lance Quinn**
Singles: **'Runaway', 'She Don't Know Me', 'Burning for Love'**

"I was 14 when this was released, been a big fan ever since and I'm 49 in August.
I'm a grandmother of three and I'm going to rock with the boys in Dublin, Ireland in 15 days time on their 'This House Is Not For Sale' tour. Woo-hoo!"
Pamela Halliday (Carrickfergus, Northern Ireland, UK)

"I love this album.
I was 15 when I first fell in love with Bon Jovi and their music."
Sarah Miles (Linford, Essex, UK)

"This is the song that made me fall in love with this BAND and there was no turning back and it's been 35 years!
I was walking down the hall MTV was on I stop in my tracks and ask my sister "WHO IS THAT?" She said "Bon Jovi" - there was no hope for me after that you stole my heart, but I ain't complaining!"
Buggy Reid (Fountain Inn, South Carolina, USA)

"Possibly my favorite album."
Michelle A. Wells (Erving, Massachusetts, USA)

"There are no words to be able to express the band from its beginning until now, they are an icon of music.
I adore them and much more, as great people."
Norma Machado (Paraná, Argentina)

"Great album. As is all the CDs that have been released."
Diane Lindsay (Worthing, UK)

"Well 35 years ago 'Runaway' it was recorded in 1981 by Power station then The Wild Ones and Southside Johnny, then he became Jon Bon Jovi in 1983 and I loved the song and thought the video was awesome.
Watched it over and over - fell in love with Jon, he was so cute with that long hair fine body and his face was perfect and the most beautiful smile ever seen.
I have always loved every song he wrote and didn't write but he sang them all and I loved each one of them.
Jon has a heart of gold and helps everybody in need he is the greatest ever! That what I can remember off the top of my head for now love JBJ!!"
Janet Dean Abernathy (Cartersville, Georgia, USA)

"Love this album."
Lynne Reid (Glasgow, UK)

"Man I'm old. I love this Album."
Buddy Reid (Fountain Inn, South Carolina, USA)

"Love the album, the band. And of course love Jon! Die-hard fan!!"
Debbie Ford (USA)

"I love this album.
I was 15 when I first fell in love with Bon Jovi and their music - which was the 'Slippery When Wet' era.
I've then gone back and got all their previous albums and now have the full collection and more. Their music has been with me all of my life, through the good times and has helped me through the bad times.
I've seen the band live every time they have come to the UK.
I'm 44 now and I love them as much as I did when I was 15.
I even had them tattooed on me."
Sarah Miles (Linford, Essex, UK)

SARAH MILES

"Confession time, my brother had borrowed this tape and had it in his car. For some reason I looked at the name and then the cover and thought they were French (the Bon threw me).

It lasted a few songs and then I put something else on. I gave it another go and thought "actually, this is good."

The 'love affair' began, they supported Kiss in '84 and I saw half their show, as our coach was late.

I made up for it on the following tours though."
David Jones (Warsop, UK)

Argentina

(Including My Favourite Concert)

"Buenos Aires, Argentina 2010. I was there..."
Juan Fernandez (Lomas de Zamora, Argentina)

Estadio River Plate, Buenos Aires
3rd October 2010
'The Circle' Tour

Blood on Blood
We Weren't Born to Follow
You Give Love a Bad Name
Lost Highway
In These Arms
Captain Crash & the Beauty Queen from Mars
Who Says You Can't Go Home

Superman Tonight
We Got It Goin' On
It's My Life
Bad Medicine
Lay Your Hands on Me
Always
Blaze of Glory
I'll Be There for You
Raise Your Hands
Runaway
I'll Sleep When I'm Dead
Keep the Faith
Dry County
Wanted Dead or Alive
Livin' on a Prayer
These Days
Have a Nice Day
Someday I'll Be Saturday Night
Bed of Roses

7800° Fahrenheit

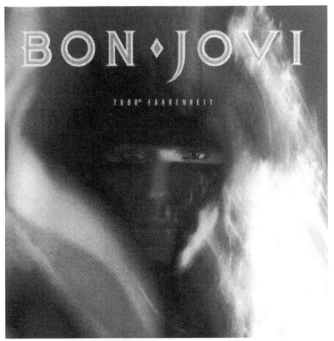

1) In and Out of Love..................4:25
2) The Price of Love...................4:14
3) Only Lonely.........................4:58
4) King of the Mountain...............3:54
5) Silent Night........................5:07
6) Tokyo Road..........................5:40
7) The Hardest Part is the Night......4:25
8) Always Run to You..................5:00
9) To the Fire.........................4:27
10) Secret Dreams......................4:56

Release Date: 27ᵗʰ March 1985
Producer: Lance Quinn
Singles: 'Only Lonely', 'In and Out of Love',
'The Hardest Part is the Night',
'Silent Night', 'The Price of Love' (Japan)

*"First heard Bon Jovi in 1989 when my brother had '**Livin' on a Prayer**' blaring out.*

Said goodbye to Jason Donovan and began my 30 year love affair with the boys. Their music has been the anthem of my life with every stage memorialised by one of their albums.

My son is now a fan and their music will live on through this next generation.

*'**Silent Night**' has to be one of my favourites and is on the '**7800 Fahrenheit**' album, which is a cracking album and is Bon Jovi at their best.*

I'm off to my 8th concert this year and I'm hoping for one wild night!!! Keep the hits coming boys, Bon Jovi till I die!!"

Rebekah Searle (UK)

"This is one of my fav albums.

*I'd love to hear '**Silent Night**' live... just one more time, but it won't happen. I once had a sign for this one. Jon saw it, just smiled and shook his head no.*

*'**In and Out of Love**' was sound checked a few years ago, so there might be hope yet for that one to be played again.*

*Unfortunately, there are a lot of painful memories connected to this for most of the band members and especially Jon, as this was the timeframe when he and Dorothea had broken up. As soon as '**Slippery When Wet**' came out, songs from '7800...' disappeared from the set list.*

It was the only record recorded in Philadelphia at the old Warehouse studio by Obie & Lance Quinn."

Margaret Farr (Brampton, Ontario, Canada)

*"The '**7800° Fahrenheit**' album was my first introduction to Bon jovi at the age of sixteen and I've never looked back.*
It is such a great iconic album, with great songs."
Fern Marlborough (In the World)

"Love this album."
Nicole Brugh (Buchanan, Michigan, USA)

"It's good."
Dacia Compton (Taylorville, Illinois, USA)

Australia

(Including My Favourite Concert)

"An absolutely exciting & phenomenal band is Bon Jovi from New Jersey.

To have grown up in the eighties listening to and watching MTV videos of their amazing songs has been an Epic time in my life. It continues to this day!

Jon and the band visited my home town of Melbourne, Australia to perform a series of concerts for the 'Slippery When Wet Tour' in September of 1987.

'Bad Name...', 'I'd Die For You' and 'Never Say Goodbye' were the standout songs for me.

In my diary that night I wrote –

"Couldn't wait until tonite 'BON JOVI NIGHT' I drove myself, Shane, Linda and Meagan to the Entertainment Centre where we saw the great Bon Jovi in concert and I tell you they were fabulous!!!

He (Jon) is SO adorable, enjoyed every minute of the concert.

A fantastic feeling of being in the same room, singing along to the songs. We had great seats too which made things even better!

Will never forget Jon flying on the wire above our heads, his captains hat & USA flag worn as a Superhero's cape."

I still love Jon and attended their latest 2018 MCG Melbourne concert (my 5th one) along with my sisters, niece and a 70,000 strong crowd!"

Sharron Archer (Mornington, Victoria, Australia)

Sports & Entertainment Centre, Melbourne, 9th September 1987 'Slippery When Wet' Tour

Pink Flamingos
Raise Your Hands
I'd Die for You
Tokyo Road
You Give Love a Bad Name
Wild in the Streets
Twist and Shout
Never Say Goodbye
Livin' on a Prayer
Let It Rock
Get Ready
Runaway
Wanted Dead or Alive
Drift Away
Travelin' Band

"In December Sydney Australia in 2010 with my friend and we absolutely loved every single bit of his concert, I even had a little cry on my friends shoulder when he came on stage and said his first words.
I was in absolute awe of his voice, I have been a big fan of his since 1985 and I have all of his CDs.
I would love to see him again if he comes back to Australia and I would love to get a photo of him with myself and my friend."
Helen Bailey (Australia)

"Love everything they do."
Bernadette Short (Port Augusta, Australia)

*"**This House Is Not for Sale**' concert, Adelaide, S.A., 4th December 2018. So Awesome."*
Lin Hattam (Tailem Bend, Australia)

"1st December 2018 Melbourne MCG. Unreal."
Wendy Buckley (Australia)

"Sydney, Australia, 2011."
Susan Mackenzie (Cairns, Australia)

*"Melbourne Australia!!! "1987" '**Slippery When Wet**' tour."*
Stav Gliatus (Melbourne, Victoria)

*"December 4th Botanic Park. Adelaide S.A. '**This House Is Not for Sale**'.*
AWESOME show. Jon, David & Tico look better now.
Jon is still a great dancer."
Lin Hattam (Tailem Bend)

*"I have been a fan since the first time I heard '**Runaway**'.*
I'm a year younger than JBJ so I've been a huge fan nearly all of my adult life.
They have come to Australia many times but I was never in a position to go to a concert until 2018.
Wow, was I excited and the guys did not disappoint; I felt so energized as if I was back in my twenties again! It was an amazing experience.
The surrounding audience consisted of kids of all ages, adults and oldies and was culturally diverse, all singing as loud as possible along with Jon.
I hope they continue well into the future spreading their unique sound, music and lyrics.
Wow, just WOW!"
Jo Kingston (Melbourne, Australia)

"I'm a big fan. They came to Australia in 1987 and I saw them."
Tony Holdsworth (Goodna, Queensland)

"December the 4th 2018 Adelaide South Australia.
I have seen Bon Jovi many times, but this was my favourite as it was the first time I took my son.
He loved it.
And they played a lot of older stuff that I have always loved. 30 years of pure joy. I was 11 when I first heard them, been a fan ever since."
Stephanie Tugwood (Australia)

"Bon Jovi came out exactly when I needed them the most in life which was when my brother died when I was 16.

I would sing their lyrics and really believe them that life would get better. Also singing out all my different emotions has always helped me.

I learn more about God from Bon Jovi than all the pastors I have seen put together. Singing keep the faith truly gave me faith.

They have always been my idols and I love absolutely everything about them. The singing, the lyrics, the music, there souls the way they are with fans, the charity work, work ethic, the looks, the videos, the concerts etc. They have helped me and the world so much in so many ways."

Gillian Woolcock (Adelaide)

"Favourite concert memory was from Rod Laver Arena 2010 in Melbourne.

Packed to the rafters, small venue and had my $90 ticket upgraded to Diamond class just for asking fab guy at ticket desk if there was a better view than back of the stage. Unforgettable night for sure!"

Sharron Archer (Mornington, Victoria)

"I have been to only two as I live in Australia.
'The Circle' tour was awesome. The Best Bon Jovi DVD in the world is
'This Left Feels Right'."
Katrina Righton (Australia)

Slippery When Wet

1) Let It Rock...............................5:26
2) You Give Love a Bad Name...........3:43
3) Livin' on a Prayer......................4:09
4) Social Disease..........................4:18
5) Wanted Dead or Alive..................5:09
6) Raise Your Hands.......................4:17
7) Without Love............................3:31
8) I'd Die for You..........................4:31
9) Never Say Goodbye....................4:49
10) Wild in the Streets....................3:56

Release Date: 18th August 1986
Producer: Bruce Fairbairn
Singles: 'You Give Love a Bad Name',
'Livin' on a Prayer', 'Wanted Dead or Alive',
'Never Say Goodbye'

*"**Slippery When Wet**' - this is the one that got my attention.*
*The first time I heard Bon Jovi was back in the day when MTV played videos non-stop. The song was '**You Give Love a Bad Name**'. Soon it was followed by '**Wanted Dead or Alive**'. I've been a fan every since."*
Dee Smith (In the World)

"Amazing album."
Julie Tyson (UK)

*"I totally remember a lot of the songs on '**Slippery When Wet**' but didn't really fall in love with Jon until January of 2002. But I made up for lost time and have now seen him in concert 90 times plus a lot of Soul Games. I have had the time of my life! Hoping for 10 more in 2020."*
Nancy Rossman (Glen Burnie, Maryland, USA)

"This was the album that inspired my whole life.
It made me want to be a guitar player and write my own songs. This album is the reason still to this day that Bon Jovi is my favorite band."
Scott Brittain (Brevard, North Carolina, USA)

*"**Slippery When Wet**' taught the world what Bon Jovi fans already knew: 'they are a force to be reckoned with'.*
I've had the pleasure of attending many concerts and Soul Games in Philly over the years. And I've also been afforded lasting friendships due to our common love of the band.
It's more than just fans: it's family."
Sherri Johnson Riddle (USA)

"One of the first albums I ever bought, still play it on CD in my car."
Cecile Bourque (Clare, Nova Scotia, Canada)

"This album totally hooked my on the boys.
The songs spoke to me and to this day still give me chills!!
They are a timeless band who have stood the test of time. They are genuine and amazing to their fans. Nothing gives me chill more than seeing them all lined up on the edge of the stage at the end of a concert soaking it all in and appreciating their fans.
Thank you Bon Jovi for always being there and being true to who you are."
Deb Wand (Kitchener, Ontario, Canada)

"My band of all time xx."
Marjorie Rhodes (Adelaide, Australia)

"This is the best album of all of them. This is the one that got me hooked for life."
Fawn Columbus (Morgan, Minnesota, USA)

"This is the album that got me hooked on the best band in the world as a 15 year old girl. Mad for them then, mad for them now.
Their tours are always great, selling out the world over. In a couple of weeks going to see them rock out again, twice, I am so excited - can't wait. I only wish they toured more often.
Love Jon Bon Jovi and he is looking great."
Sandra Wigley (Cranwell, UK)

"Best album ever."
Beth Carroll Jessen (Bayone, New Jersey, USA)

"When this album was released I was only 9!
*'**Never Say Goodbye**' is the track I fell in love to Bon Jovi at the age of 11 after hearing a high school friend play this album.*
I then became obsessed.
*I got our next-door neighbour to record some videos from SKY for me of Bon Jovi as we didn't have it back then. And then hid the VHS away from mum and dad so they couldn't record over it. I think there was only 2 possibly 3 videos on that whole tape! '**Never Say Goodbye**' being one of them, and that was it.*
I'll be seeing them at Wembley in 16 days with my daughter who has grown up listening to them with me. This will be her first time hearing and seeing them live. And I can't wait.
Thank you for the ride, and Never Stop been there for us."
Charlie Jury (Ilfracombe, UK)

"Great album."
Kevin Perkis (New York, USA)

*"**Slippery When Wet**' first introduced the guys to me.*
*We had just gotten our cable hooked up in 1986 and I fell in love with the video for '**Livin' On A Prayer**'. It was awesome!*
*They were still playing '**Shot Through The Heart**', also, double awesome!"*
Rita Mastin Stephens (Ashland, Kentucky, USA)

"I became a fan with this album, we were in the US and heard it on MTV and fell in love straight away. Bought the first 2 albums and then I was hooked."
Susanna Ekdahl (Grillby, Sweden)

*"**Slippery When Wet**' is my fav album!*
Saw Bon Jovi for the first time on this tour in Ft Wayne, Indiana !! I fell in love with JBJ then and the love continues to this day."
Kim Foust Whitney (Fort Wayne, Indiana, USA)

Austria

(Including My Favourite Concert)

"95 in Zeltweg, Austria."
Bettina Hochreiter (Gaming, Niederösterreich)

Österreich-Ring, Zeltweg, Austria, 11ᵗʰ June 1995 'These Days' Tour

Living on a Prayer
You Give Love a Bad Name
Wild in the Streets
Keep the Faith
Blood on Blood
Can't Help Falling in Love
Always
I'd Die for You
Blaze of Glory
I Believe
Runaway
Dry County

Lay Your Hands on Me
I'll Sleep When I'm Dead
Bad Medicine
Bed of Roses
Hey God
Rockin' All Over the World
Wanted Dead or Alive
Someday I'll Be Saturday Night

New Jersey

1) Lay Your Hands on Me................5:58
2) Bad Medicine.........................5:16
3) Born to Be My Baby.................4:40
4) Living in Sin..........................4:39
5) Blood on Blood.....................6:16
6) Homebound Train..................5:10
7) Wild Is the Wind....................5:08
8) Ride Cowboy Ride...................1:25
9) Stick to Your Guns..................4:45
10) I'll Be There for You.................5:46
11) 99 in the Shade......................4:29
12) Love for Sale........................3:58

Release Date: 19th September 1988

Producer: **Bruce Fairbairn**

Singles: **'Bad Medicine', ' Born to Be My Baby', 'I'll Be There for You', 'Lay Your Hands on Me', 'Living in Sin'**

"This one is 'hands down' my husbands favorite, it is the only album he will admit to loving...
I found him an original vinyl for Christmas."
DeAnne Lynnette (USA)

"Love."
Maria Francisca (São Pedro do Piauí, Brazil)

"In my opinion the best album they did, love it, might get on exercise bike later and put it on.
Looking forward to seeing them on Sunday, playing the classics from this album."
Nick Allen (Gloucester, UK)

"About 'New Jersey' - the video for the song, 'I'll Be There for You' was on heavy rotation on MTV while I was in college.
My roommate and our two next-door neighbors visited one another frequently, and MTV was on a great deal of the time.
When 'I'll Be There for You' came on, no one spoke. We would listen and stare at the TV as if we were mesmerized and no one would dare speak! What a fun memory."
Melissa Martin Collins (USA)

"Absolutely wonderful, what an amazing performer."
Denise Sicard (In the World)

"The album!"
Amaia Olazabal (Algorta, Spain)

"I have all of his CD's and he is the best ever and has saved me so many time's. Love him so much."
Hope Green (Carrollton, Georgia, USA)

"Me too ♥."
Marina Coosemans (Belgium)

"I have that CD."
Billie Howell (USA)

"Brilliant!"
Naomi Booker (In the World)

"I LOVE this album.
Got the cassette as a gift when I was 13 years old and loved singing **'I'll Be There for You'** *with my hairbrush.*
Eventually the tape recorder ate my cassette, which was heartbreaking!
But a few years back I managed to get the deluxe CD!
All the songs on here have a memory attached for me."
Natasha Fester (Cape Town, South Africa)

"Never get tired of listening to this album."
Joel Devardhi (Hyderabad, India)

"I have this original CD."
Neuza Rosmaninho (Brazil)

"The most of the most!"
Maritxu Aydi (In the World)

*"***Stick to Your Guns***' is still my crie song."*
Tonny Cristin Jensen (Oslo, Norway)

"I love this album and all songs on it."
Joan Mosher (West Hurley, New York, USA)

"I remember this album so well!
I was given this by my now husband - but at the time my boyfriend - for
my 17 birthday. He knew I loved the band.
So we decided when we got married that our dance song had to be 'I'll
Be There for You'."
Julie Brown (Green Bay, Wisconsin, USA)

"Got this CD."
Ju Silva (Carapicuíba, Brazil)

"I loved this album played it all the time. Still play it mark of great music
in my opinion."
Donna Klimcho (USA)

"I got the tape and CD."
Holly Royston (USA)

"My first album, my first concert, Birmingham NEC. Still in love."
Karen Wilson (Truro, Cornwall, UK)

Belgium

(Including My Favourite Concert)

"The best of the best was the 1st night of Wembley 1995. This yeah was very special. We were at the 1st row in Wembley Stadium... amazing."
Nadine Massart (Zaventem, Belgium)

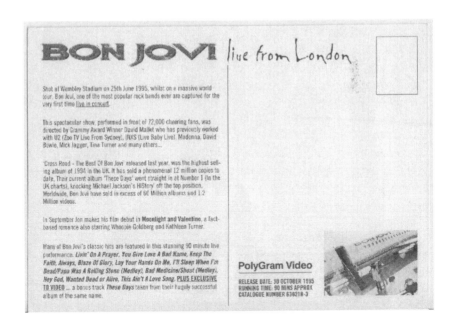

Canada

(Including My Favourite Concert)

"I would have to say 1983, the only one the two of us attended, lmao but boy what a show."
Jill Dezsenyi (Canada)

"Private message of encouragement when l was starting out on Facebook - Highlight in my Life from Jon and Bon Jovi.
I love every song ever created. This band and Jon's band now' brilliant."
Laurie Lynn Barill (Canada)

"2005 in New Jersey."
Sheila Rissis (Markham, Ontario)

"I have been a huge Bon Jovi fan since I heard the song 'Runaway'.
I love the song 'Always', as well as the song 'Thank You For Loving Me'.
I haven't seen him in concert yet, but I will someday. I think that he is so talented and I really want to see him in concert he is not only an amazing musician he is also involved in charity work I would fly just about anywhere to see him in concert love the man and his music very much."
Lena Farrell (Sydney, Nova Scotia, Canada)

"I was about 3 years old at the time, my Uncle would babysit me.

*We'd rock out to '**Runaway**' album played on a record player. We'd dance and we'd sing.*

I don't remember a time when Bon Jovi wasn't my all time favourite, and I don't see there ever being a time they are not. Over the years there's been some changes, they've said goodbyes, and they said hello. Growing up on the Northern Peninsula of Newfoundland my life long dream was to get to see them live in concert - well let me tell you!!

Skipping ahead to 2005, I'm currently living in Kitchener Ontario. It's 8:30 am I'm in the shower getting ready for work in Guelph that starts at 9:30 when the phone rings.

It's my team teacher Tasha (we worked in childcare as ECE's) she's saying tickets go on sale at 9 for Bon Jovi in Toronto that coming January. Because I don't have time to wait until 9 at home, and still get to work on time. I jumped out of the shower half-dress and take whatever else I needed to get ready. I cut the half hour drive to work down to 15 minutes and make it with a few minutes to spare.

We've got the special pre-sale code and we are golden.

So many people are trying to buy tickets the system is being a pain. We didn't get our tickets before I started work, but we've got friends. Our peeps keep working on it until, voila we have three tickets to see Bon Jovi on January 21, 2006.

Now let's skip to January, it's been a few sleepless nights leading up to the most exciting day of my life, the day I get to stand in the same room as my idol Jon Bongiovi.

I am out of bed it's super early when the phone rings, I answer it's my cousins wife. She is explaining how the show is cancelled because their plane had gone off the runway in Hamilton. She said my cousin had heard it on the radio but couldn't bring himself to telling me because he knew I'd be heartbroken. I was so scared because I didn't know how the guys were, if they'd gotten hurt.

I called Tasha and she got upset, we were trying to call the ACC to see if they knew anything, but they were not open yet. Finally Tasha called her Mom, who in turn blamed her brother for getting her upset (they had heard it, but they also heard everyone was ok, but her brother said he was going to just tell her about the plane off the runway part to get her worked up, but he didn't).

She confirmed the plane had just skidded off the runway but the guys were all well and the show was still going as planned.

We are finally off to Toronto.

We eat in a restaurant that's playing Bon Jovi the whole time.

We are off to the ACC, it's super early we sit in our amazing seats just 10 rows from the right stage, but there's a side stage that comes up almost to our row. My whole body shaking I'm so excited, it's very difficult to hold back the happy tears.

The stadium starts to fill, Daughtry (who is amazing as well does their set.).

Patiently waiting tears are close to my lids, the lights go low out walks Richie, David and Tico, I can't handle much more then it happens... Out walks Jon my heart over flows and I just lose it.

I sang and I cried I just couldn't handle the excitement. I calmed down as the show went on, I always look back and laugh because I saw when he was on the stage near us he flicked his hair and a drop of his sweat hit me.

*I was doing pretty good until the music started playing, it was '**Bed of Roses**'. I again started to tear up as I listened to this beautiful man sing my all time favourite song.*

That day has gone down in my history as the day one of my dreams came true.

After that experience I decided I needed to see them play a home show in Jersey. So a couple more concerts under our belts and voila tickets to see them play Giants Stadium.

We made a road trip out of it.

We visited Jon's hometown, went to his old high school where he met the love of his life (one of the reasons I have so much respect for him is his loyalty and dedication to Dorothea and their 4 kids). Then we headed to Red Bank to visit the restaurant that The Jon Bon Jovi Foundation had created to allow the less fortunate a place to have a nice meal. The Soul Kitchen, unfortunately the kitchen wasn't open so we didn't get to eat there, but we did meet the manager and a staff member. The manager told us how Jon and the family come and help out when they can, and when he's there the manager is the boss and Jon follows his directions. The staff member who was a dishwasher told us how he once lived on the streets, he had came into the restaurant to get a meal once and offered to wash dishes to pay off his meal, when he was offered a job. He was currently living in an apartment because the Soul Kitchen gave a homeless man the opportunity to prove himself. He told us how when Jon comes in he treats everyone with the most upmost respect. The dishwasher is just as important as the cook or the people who can afford to pay full price. (Another reason my love and respect for Jon is so deep, his respect for everyone).

I'm 13 shows in and hope that number keeps growing. My new dream is to get to meet Jon, shake his hand have a photo or two and get him to

autograph my wrist or shoulder so I can get it tattooed along with a rose to symbolize 'Bed of Roses'.
I will forever Love and Respect all that is Bon Jovi. Sorry for long winded story I could honestly go on forever, I have special stories for each show."
Joanne Quinlan (Cook Harbour, Canada)

Air Canada Centre, Toronto
'Have A Nice Day' Tour
21st January 2006

Last Man Standing
You Give Love a Bad Name
I'll Sleep When I'm Dead
Runaway
Just Older
Complicated
Born to Be My Baby
Story of My Life
Wild Is the Wind
Novocaine
I Won't Back Down
Have a Nice Day
Who Says You Can't Go Home
It's My Life
I'll Be There for You
Blaze of Glory
Bed of Roses
Bad Medicine
Raise Your Hands
Livin' on a Prayer
Welcome to Wherever You Are
Blood on Blood
Keep the Faith
Wanted Dead or Alive
Treat Her Right

*"Barcelona when I won the trip to see the guys in concert. Heard them sing '**Bed of Roses**' in Spanish."*
Andrea Gibbons (Oshawa, Ontario)

"Jon Bon Jovi, love you too so much."
Tara Pretty (Canada)

"Hope to see him in Montréal, Québec Canada again this year."
Denise Sicard (Canada)

"Ottawa, Ontario, Canada May 03, 2011... the night Jon tossed me his maraccas.
It was also the first time I saw Phil X play with the band."
Margaret Farr (Brampton, Ontario)

"Fans should just be nicer to each other. I am tired of being the nicest person in the bunch & getting excluded."
Afsha Bee (Canada)

"Montréal. August 1995.
I was a young teenager who was learning to play guitar. When the band came on stage and I heard the crowd, I knew at that moment that I was living something special.
*When I heard Richie's Fender in '**Dry County**', my heart just stopped beating.*
Then, when you hear:
"Oh, we're half way there. Oh, oh, livin' on a prayer!"
You Just know that your life will never be the same!"
Claude Castonguay (Quebec)

*"Bon Jovi's '**Slippery When Wet**' album was released when I was 12 years old! My Dad was a Grade 8 teacher and had to preview the songs that would be played at the school dances! I fell in love with the songs as soon as the first chord of the album struck!*
June 2nd, 1989 was my first chance to see the band live in Toronto, Ontario Canada! It was my first concert ever. As soon as the band took the stage at the CNE I was mesmerized. It was like magic! Jon's stage presence was amazing! Since then I have followed their career and seen the band live over 50 times in Canada, the States and in the UK!
I will be a fan 'til the day that I die!"
Shell Adams (Canada)

"Out-door concert in Montreal."
Vito Sacchetti (Canada)

*"My best memory of '**THINFS**' tour was dancing in the audience to '**Bed of Roses**' while Jon sang to us all...*
It was so magical we are the real 'Tommy and Gina'.
Oh I forgot to add... caught that tour both times but the last show was most memorable (Toronto Feb 2018) - Jon you never disappoint..."
Tammy Aalders (Toronto, Canada)

"All of them are memorable, but I think New York, the opening of Met Life Stadium in May 2010, 3 shows and sound check.
The energy was amazing. Another that stands out is Calgary when Richie failed to show up, that one stands out, I felt so bad for the band, but they rocked it and next day in Edmonton, Phil X did a great job."
Brenda Goff (Regina, Saskatchewan)

Keep the Faith

1) I Believe.................................5:52
2) Keep the Faith...........................5:46
3) I'll Sleep When I'm Dead.................4:43
4) In These Arms...........................5:20
5) Bed of Roses............................6:34
6) If I Was Your Mother....................4:27
7) Dry County..............................9:52
8) Woman in Love...........................3:50
9) Fear....................................3:07
10) I Want You.............................5:36
11) Blame It on the Love of Rock & Roll....4:24
12) Little Bit of Soul.....................5:44
13) Save a Prayer..........................5:57

Release Date: 3ʳᵈ November 1992
Producer: Bob Rock
Singles: 'Keep the Faith', 'Bed of Roses'
'In These Arms', 'I'll Sleep When I'm Dead',
'I Believe', 'Dry County'

"Beautiful single."
Mary Flores (São Paulo, Brazil)

"Yes, yes, yes."
Denise Sicard (Greece)

"Good 'come back album' especially after they split after 'New Jersey' album. Really good album glad they all worked out differences."
Harrison Caraballo Jr. (USA)

"This album helped me through a lot of issues & a new marriage."
Debbie Ford (USA)

"So many amazing songs, best album."
Christine Berish (North Cambria, Pennsylvania, USA)

"Absolutely adore this album, I never get bored of listening to it and if it is after a while the songs always sound fresh and new to me.
Wish they would write more albums like this."
Aileen Langtry-Palmer (Mansfield, UK)

"This is a brilliant album."
Julie Tyson (UK)

"One of the best ones."
Elisa Theriault (Moncton, New Brunswick, Canada)

"Such a great album and 'Keep The Faith' is something I say regularly to those who are going thru difficult times. They are appreciative of course, and chuckle when I say its a Bon Jovi song - cause most of them know of my obsession...lol."
Pam Barrett (USA)

"Love this album."
Fawn Columbus (Morgan, Minnesota, USA)

"My first vinyl record."
Natalia Abdo Commodaro (Pedregulho, São Paulo, Brazil)

"I think we all have it."
Ferry Luijendijk (Netherlands)

"I absolutely love this album!"
Denise McKinley (North Myrtle Beach, South Carolina, USA)

"Great album."
Bernie Stevens (Sunbury-on-Thames, UK)

"I have this one."
Aldair Santos (Belo Horizonte, Brazil)

"Best album ever!!"
Alexandra Jeukens (Emmeloord, Netherlands)

"Hugs."
Monalisa Hughes (Hamilton, Ontario, Canada)

"I like this album. Also... I really like all Bon Jovi songs..."
Abdulio Cuba (Dumaguete City, Philippines)

"Tremendous album!!"
Soraya Amut (Tandil, Argentina)

"I love that picture, it says a lot a bout the best band ever."
Kristen Staffian (USA)

"I like this Bon Jovi."
Anton Fernandez (Dagupan, Philippines)

"This was one of my best albums of all times. Helped me through a lot."
Kimberley Stuart (UK)

*"I've loved Bon Jovi since '83 (I was 18) this particular album came out a year before my youngest son was born, and I find it amazing that one of his favorite songs is '**Lay Your Hands On Me**'.*
Personally I can't pick a favorite, so many songs are like telling my life story.
My husband and I even called each other Tommy and Gina!
I'm a die hard Bon Jovi fan till I die!"
Kelly Terry (USA)

Croatia

(Including My Favourite Concert)

"Starting from beginning, there isn't much of a story, since I am young and been fan for a couple of years.

I first heard them when I was 11 years old, 10 and a half years ago, my mom introduced me to Bon Jovi world and I am so thankful for that.

I only saw them once, in Germany. It was in 2013, 'Because We Can' tour, city was Cologne, and it was June 22, Saturday.

The most amazing day in my life without a doubt. I was so far away from stage but it didn't matter at all.

I travelled from Croatia just to see them live. Playlist was amazing, they were amazing, they even replied to me on Twitter couple days later.

I am still huge huge fan, and for sure I will always be.

No one like Bon Jovi."

Antonija Buzov (Solin, Croatia)

Czech Republic

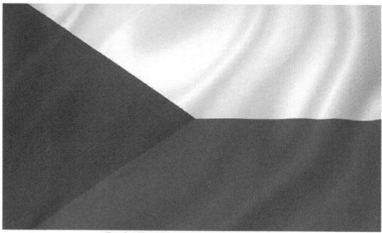

(Including My Favourite Concert)

*"Wembley 1995 and '**Lost Highway**' Chicago 2007."*
Jan Vytásek (Prague, Czech Republic)

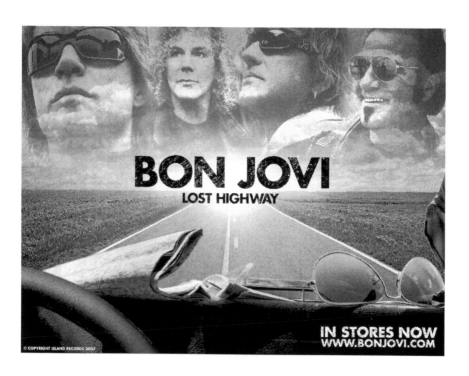

Cross Road

1) Livin' on a Prayer......................4:11
2) Keep the Faith.........................5:45
3) Someday I'll Be Saturday Night........4:38
4) Always................................5:52
5) Wanted Dead or Alive..................5:07
6) Lay Your Hands on Me..................5:58
7) You Give Love a Bad Name..............3:43
8) Bed of Roses..........................6:34
9) Blaze of Glory........................5:40
10) In These Arms........................5:16
11) Bad Medicine.........................5:14
12) I'll Be There for You................5:41
13) In and Out of Love...................4:23
14) Runaway..............................3:50

Release Date: 11th October 1994
Producer: Tony Bongiovi, Jon Bon Jovi, Richie Sambora, Bruce Fairbairn, Bob Rock, Peter Collins, Danny Kortchmar, Lance Quinn
Singles: 'Always', 'Someday I'll Be Saturday Night'

"I was married in a very abusive marriage with 3 small children.
I always liked Bon Jovi but until 'Cross Road' came out, and I listened to it a thousand times, I fell in love with them from that point.
Now if I'm in a bad place I listen to 'Saturday Night...' and it always lifts my spirits.
Bon Jovi forever!"
Lynne Evans (Mountain Ash, Wales, UK)

"Great."
Marjorie Rhodes (Australia)

"Just well chosen tracks. An album to have on repeat."
Donna Brimson (Portsmouth, UK)

"I was 15 when 'Cross Road' was released.
'Always' was the song that started my forever love for Bon Jovi.
2 years later I went to my first Bon Jovi concert, I was hooked!!
Now 25 years later, I have seen them 9 times. And have even managed to get front row a few times.
I am now passing my love for Bon Jovi down to my two sons. They love them almost as much as me."
Serena Taylor (Shepton Mallet, UK)

"'Always' - My favourite of all time."
Yvonne Lovering (Plymouth, UK)

"When you're a 13 year old and hear 'You Give Love a Bad Name' on the radio, it's like a drug.
Instantly different to everything I was brought up on.
Now have every CD, some concert DVD and have seen them several times.
Even now they are still the biggest and best band on planet earth.
Bon Jovi until I die."
Robin 'Shakespeare' Grigsby (Teynham, UK)

"This one I have."
Aldair Santos (Belo Horizonte, Brasil)

*"I call the '**Cross Road**' album, for me, 'Re-Discovery' of Bon Jovi.
It had been a busy few years, but this album reminded me of how much I
had enjoyed the music. I became a bigger fan than before at this point!"*
Melissa Martin Collins (USA)

"Easy cool."
Stefanie Keck (Germany)

"Love the CD."
Monalisa Hughes (St. Johns, Canada)

*"One of my favorites on this CD is '**Someday I'll be Saturday Night**'.
Love the entire CD!"*
Regina Duren (Humble, Texas, USA)

"I have set this CD up a lot."
Veronique Laporte (In the World)

"Love the CD."
Monalisa Hughes (St. Johns, Canada)

"I've always liked Bon Jovi since first song.
Raised my kids with there music.
Had the opportunity's to meet when I worked Security at the old Wembley
in London 1994/95. Was fab, glorious.
I'm a forever fan of the guys and their brill music. Always in my heart.
Keep up the good work guys. Love and Light to ya all..."
Kimberley Stuart (UK)

*"**Cross Road**" album - that is my absolute favourite love every single*
song on there, the man is a legend.
I listening to him since I was 3 and I'm 30 this year - shows how good he
is.
My first concert was Anfield 2019 and omg it was phenomenal.
My 4-year listens to him and loves him he's been listening since he was 3
as well, like mother like son."
Louise Clark (UK)

Denmark

(Including My Favourite Concert)

"I'm went to my first one in 2008 in Denmark.
It was a culmination of a stressful day where traffic problems, which made us nervous that we wouldn't make in time and it had been raining all afternoon.
But we made it in good time and the rain had stopped.
The show was fantastic with a great set-list and the band was on top of their game.
*'**I'll Be There For You**' with Richie and '**Always**' where the highlights."*
Jesper Pedersen (Galten)

Germany

(Including My Favourite Concert)

"Best band in the world for me.
Your music has accompanied me through every day and every darkness, for many years. They give me the feeling of being not alone.
They are my family, through them I don't grow up without a family. They give so much power in this loneliness Thank you guys.
There is really not a day your music is not playing. It is as important as the air to breathe. Without your music, I wouldn't be complete anymore, so I know that your music will always run until my last breath - every day because through your music we fans all get better air, she cleans the fog of life.
'It's my life It's now or never I ain't gonna live forever, I just want to listen to Bon Jovi while I'm alive'.
Wish you and your family's/friend's only the best for the future."
Hannah (Germany)

"That's really nice to express what I personally am for a Bon Jovi fan.
Not a day passes where I do not hear his great music.
He is the greatest musician for me ever.
I saw Bon Jovi in Hamburg and it was great. "
Brigitte Grage (Lübeck, Germany)

These Days

1) Hey God................................6:03
2) Something for the Pain..................4:46
3) This Ain't a Love Song..................5:06
4) These Days.............................6:26
5) Lie to Me..............................5:34
6) Damned................................4:35
7) My Guitar Lies Bleeding in My Arms......5:42
8) (It's Hard) Letting You Go.............5:50
9) Hearts Breaking Even...................5:05
10) Something to Believe In................5:25
11) If That's What It Takes...............5:17
12) Diamond Ring..........................3:46
13) All I Want Is Everything..............5:18
14) Bitter Wine...........................4:36

Release Date: 27th June 1995
Producer: Jon Bon Jovi, Richie Sambora, Peter Collins
Singles: 'This Ain't a Love Song',
'Something for the Pain', 'Lie to Me',
'These Days', 'Hey God'

"My favourite album of all time!!
I discovered Bon Jovi when I was 11 and I've been a fan ever since.
This album literally carried me through my last years of high school, it was my go to album and when I felt I had nothing to believe in, they gave me something to believe in.
This album was darker than their previous work but I love it as it connected with me in a way that no other artist has ever done or ever will.
This album still connects with me as if it were the first time I had heard it. The best album to date."
Kelly Wheeler (Cowes, Isle of Wight, UK)

*"**These Days**'... I thought was a very grown up album with some fantastic songs on it. In my eyes this is Bon Jovi close to their prime..."*
Rob O'Brien (Brisbane, Australia)

*"13 year old me fell in love with the band when '**Keep The Faith**' was released. '**These Days**' strengthened that relationship and ever since, the Jovi guys seemed to know what was up with me and my life before I really knew, always in tune with my life journey.*
Thank you for the incredible concerts, heartfelt words and generous smiles!"
Jennifer Karos (Cologne, Germany)

"One of my favourite albums.
*When Bon Jovi play '**These Days**' live, I have flashback memories of my teenage years.*
*I also love '**Hey God**', but they don't seem to play that song live so often now.*
*Although I was into Bon Jovi at an early age in the '80s, '**These Days**' was the first album I bought by Bon Jovi."*
Tammy Meras (In the World)

*"**These Days**' is one of my faves."*
Bella Kaye Eccelston (Manchester, UK)

"Love this album, still sounds fresh."
Aileen Langtry-Palmer (UK)

"Fantastic album, listened to it over and over when I first got it, mind you I do that with all their albums, especially at night laying on the bed in the dark, you just get lost in their world.
I have and will always be one of their loving fans."
Suzanne Gardiner (Sudbury, Suffolk, UK)

"Helped me through Uni!!"
Sarah Miles (Linford, Essex)

"Hey my favourite Bon Jovi album ever.
Loved their eighties stuff but this made me a lifetime fan."
Randhir Ramsingh (In the World)

"Never say good buy.... My life's journey in 1995, best year of my
life...and Bon Jovi was with me every step of the way playing 'These
Days' over and over lol."
Glen Harmse (Johannesburg, South Africa)

"Loved this album, especially the song 'Lie To Me' cause at the time I
was going through a difficult relationship.
I also seen them in concert not long after the album came out in Antioch,
Tn at Star Wood."
Bruce Staggs (Lawrenceburg, Tennessee, USA)

"These Days' is one of their best albums in my opinion, it will always be
remembered as it was released when I first saw them at the great concert
in Wembley.
The song writing changed, showed a maturity side to the lads. An album
many people can relate too."
Sharon Power (Coralstown, Ireland)

"My joint favourite Jovi album along with 'New Jersey'.
I remember buying the tape and CD on the day of release as I couldn't
wait to get home and listen to it and was too impatient to record the CD
on to tape for the car.
I wasn't disappointed, not a bad song on the album and Bon Jovi moving
further away from their typical sound as they had started doing with
'Keep the Faith'.
Songs, solo's and lyrics to give you goosebumps on this album and they
were musically at their peak."
David Jones (Warsop, UK)

"Very deep and dark album.
Great songs with great lyrics. Showed a different side to the band.
I loved the album and it was just out when I saw them at Wembley, when
Bon Jovi were at their peak."
Robin 'Shakespeare' Grigsby (Teynham, UK)

"Love."
Yvonne Young (Cumbernauld, Scotland, UK)

"Ah, 'These Days' you good friend.
This album is my favorite not only by Bon Jovi, but by any band.
Some songs just strike a person at the right time in life. 'Something to Believe In' did that for me.
This album is so special to me."
Melissa Martin Collins (USA)

"It's the only album and the only band that has ever struck a chord with me and it still feels that way today!!"
Kelly Wheeler (Cowes, Isle of Wight, UK)

"BEST Bon Jovi album of them all!"
RuthAnn Berger (USA)

"My absolute favorite album! Each song is so special."
Marsha Marcy (USA)

"I have this CD."
Luciana Stopato (São Paulo, Brazil)

"These Days' album is 1 of Bon Jovi's best albums.
My favourite song of this album is 'If That's What It Takes' and 'Hey God' is a very close runner up.
My mum and I saw them 3 weeks ago at Wembley stadium, London for the 6th time. They still are amazing."
Victoria Sutton (London, UK)

"Their best, in my opinion, and my favourite."
Ivor Moon (In the World)

"Saved me. Saves me still."
Rochelle Collins (Melbourne, Australia)

"Front row at Olympic Stadium, Melbourne.
Back in the days when the earlier you lined up at a venue for general admission the closer you got to the front. No extreme prices for front row, just dedicated fans lining up to see their fav band.
Jon sang to me. I've since met all the band but paid big VIP prices so front row for $60 at 'These Days' tour was awesome, plus the best album in my opinion."
Jodie Harwood (Australia)

"Class album. My first and still my favourite."
Julie Pinkney Hoyle (UK)

"Got one of Tico's sticks from that tour."
Adrian Wright (Nottingham, UK)

"Great Album!"
Patricia A. Pilcher (In the World)

"This is one of my favourite all time CDs, but then again, most of his albums are really good. Can't get enough of his songs and always turn him up loud in the car."
April May (Saltford, UK)

"Best Bon Jovi CD ever! After that it was still good."
Mike Meredith (Jacksonville, Florida, USA)

"Love this one."
Michelle Bloom (USA)

*"**These Days**' is one of their best. To me it was underrated but the lyrics are just incredible!*
*Love when they sing '**These Days**' live too!!"*
Pam Barrett (USA)

"Best album of them all."
Donna Watson (UK)

"Very good album!!!
I think the song 'These Days' tells everything about this decade ('90s),
I love it!!!"
Adel Reyes (Morón, Cuba)

"One of their best albums. Melodic, memorable and fun songs."
Georgina Cantlon (Hamilton, Ontario, Canada)

France

(Including My Favourite Concert)

"Wembley 1995."
Didier Savineau (Caen, France)

In The World

(Including My Favourite Concert)

"Been a fan since 1983."
Paul Pisano (In the World)

"ALL OF THEM!!"
Patricia Battaglia (In the World)

"I just want to say that the Bon Jovi band is something magical that arrived suddenly and entered my heart when I was a teenager and I was helpless to reject them until now.
They are part of my life's journey that is too sweet to forget. They will remain in a special place in my heart, Infinity and Beyond."
Heitlaiers (In the World)

"Yesterday, today, tomorrow and always Bon Jovi."
Nuria Nuria (In the World)

Crush

1) It's My Life..3:44
2) Say It Isn't So..3:33
3) Thank You for Loving Me.............................5:09
4) Two Story Town..5:10
5) Next 100 Years...6:19
6) Just Older..4:29
7) Mystery Train..5:14
8) Save the World...5:31
9) Captain Crash & The Beauty Queen from Mars......4:31
10) She's a Mystery..5:18
11) I Got the Girl..4:36
12) One Wild Night...4:18
13) I Could Make a Living Out of Lovin' You.............4:40
14) Neurotica..4:45

Release Date: 13ᵗʰ June 2000

Producer: Jon Bon Jovi, Richie Sambora, Luke Ebbin
Singles: 'It's My Life', 'Say It Isn't So',
'Thank You for Loving Me'

"This Album got me through the worst time in my life. 2005 my younger Brother was killed in a car accident. All I can remember is listening to Bon Jovi. Thanks Guys for your amazing music."
Lin Hattam (Tailem Bend, Australia)

"This album, I have original, because the others are not original."
Izabel Quadros (Brazil)

"VERY, VERY LOVELY AMAZING ABSOLUTELY PERFECT ALBUM 'CRUSH!'
Bohdana Latalová (Czech Republic)

"Love their music and play in my car every day!
This album is timeless and still sounds relevant today!"
Georgina Cantlon (Hamilton, Ontario, Canada)

India

(Including My Favourite Concert)

"I myself has seen Bon Jovi during their 'Crossroads to the East' tour '95 at Mumbai for me that was a the greatest concert as I saw it with my own eyes.
But for the world I think Bon Jovi '95 tour at Wembley Stadium by far is the greatest all time."
Anuja Gupta (Gauhati)

One Wild Night: Live 1985-2001

1) It's My Life..............................3:50
2) Livin' on a Prayer............................5:13
3) You Give Love a Bad Name.............3:53
4) Keep the Faith...........................6:19
5) Someday I'll Be Saturday Night.........6:30
6) Rockin' in the Free World................5:45
7) Something to Believe In..................6:00
8) Wanted Dead or Alive....................5:59
9) Runaway..................................4:47
10) In and Out of Love......................6:12
11) I Don't Mondays..........................5:37
12) Just Older...............................5:13
13) Something for the Pain..................4:22
14) Bad Medicine............................4:19
15) One Wild Night..........................3:43

Release Date: 22nd May 2001
Producer: Obie O'Brien, Bon Jovi, Richie Sambora
Luke Ebbin, Desmond Child
Singles: 'One Wild Night', 'Wanted Dead or Alive'

"Best Time of the Band."
Michael Bittman (Pfeddersheim, Germany)

"This album is currently my obsession (again)."
Heather Lynn Hughes Manzella (Illinois, USA)

"YESTERDAY, TODAY, TOMORROW AND ALWAYS BON JOVI."
Nuria Nuria (Spain)

"Best songs ever x."
Jane Evans (Littlehampton, UK)

"Absolutely love this album, so many fantastic songs to choose from."
Aileen Langtry-Palmer (Mansfield, UK)

"Brilliant album."
Rachel Screen (Lydney, UK)

"Love it."
Yvonne Young (Cumbernauld, Scotland, UK)

Ireland

(Including My Favourite Concert)

"June 7th 2008 Punchetstown Co. Kildare, Ireland.
Sun was shining (for a change in Ire.), Kid Rock was so amazing too."
Sinéad Byrne (County Kildare, Ireland)

*"**Crush**' tour Dublin...*
It was thunder and lightning all night. Was an unbelievable backdrop...
Don't think Jon and the band even realised how amazing it was as most
of it was happening behind the stage.
Jon himself did mention the angels coming to the show and with that the
whole sky lit up and the thunder made an amazing racket, think he got a
fright, the timing was impeccable like he had a deal with the angels to
come in on cue!! Something I'll never forget.
I've never missed a concert here in Ireland and will be there again next
Saturday!! 6 months pregnant and ready to dance my socks off."
Lindsay Burke (Waterford, Ireland)

"I am a huge Bon Jovi fan. I am 41 years old and have loved them for 30
years.
I recently went to their concert in Dublin, Ireland (I am from Galway
which lies on the west coast). They were phenomenal. I met some of the
band in Dublin but not Jon Bon Jovi.
It is my dream to meet him so... I booked to see them in Germany when
they played there in July. Everything that COULD go wrong, DID go
wrong.
The following is an account of what happened.

My Bon Jovi Story...

On June 16th in Dublin, I went to see Bon Jovi with 2 great friends of mine. The day before the concert, I had it in my head to meet the band.

I went to the Intercontinental Hotel in Dublin (I guessed the location) and indeed I met the band, all but JBJ himself.

The concert the following night was nothing short of spectacular. 3 hours of Bon Jovi belting out their greatest hits. The stage churning out images of old Bon Jovi and the album covers relevant to the songs being played. In fairness I've never seen a more impressive set up as I did that evening. It rained, we got wet, but as one of the girls said -

"It added to the atmosphere!"

Fast forward a few weeks to the day I made a totally impulsive decision and booked a ticket to Düsseldorf, Germany to see the band I have loved for 30 years. I can't explain why - I just had to go.

I got my ticket and money together and off I went - trying to keep those who were laughing and sniggering at me to the very back of my mind. As I write this, I am sitting at a pizza place on Hammer St, Düsseldorf. The concert is over and I am reflecting on what I have learned over the past 2 days - Here it is...

I have learned the value of family and friends - from those who texted to see if I was ok and those who answered the call when I wasn't ok. To be honest, I have never done anything like this before, nor am I likely to again. I have learned that I am very much a people person - I love other people's company and I love to talk. I have never been as lonely in all my life.

I missed my husband and my dog Toby.

I learned that I am resilient.

My sandal broke (I cried), my eyes puffed shut from an allergic reaction to sun cream (I cried), the zip burst on my dress (I cried - not because the zip burst, but because I probably burst through it), I met Bon Jovi (not JBJ) (I cried). The German people that I encountered weren't nice (zero craic) -I cried. I told both Bon Jovi guitarists that they were the nicest people I have met (I cried).

I am done crying... for now. How does that show resilience? Not sure... but I'm still here living to tell the tale.

Bon Jovi as a band are amazing - the drummer Tico Torres and "on the keys, if you please" David Bryan are original members with JBJ. I'm sure they have a pain in their arse with the likes of me awkwardly 'accidentally on purpose' bumping into them asking for a photo. I met them in Dublin and didn't ask for a photo on this occasion but they obliged others. Up close, they are every inch the rock stars and wear this status with pride although age has taken its toll (on all of us).

The concert was amazing, indoors - loud as hell but totally different from Dublin. There was a different atmosphere - Dublin was better.

Later on that night I had the pleasure of chatting to JBJ's voice coach and she said Norway and Dublin were memorable for the band. The crowd were amazing! It was nice to hear!

My new best friends are Phil X, John Shanks and Hugh McDonald. They are easy breezy - snuggle in and take a photo - type people. Very down to earth and very, very kind (and I told them so - then I cried, sure 'twas all very overwhelming).

I booked in to the hotel they stayed at (cost an arm and two legs... and a kidney but as Mammy said –

"sure you could be paying it to see a consultant or to get treatment of some sort!") and I saw first hand the work that goes on behind the scenes. Counting bags, checking them off the list, making sure they were put into the relevant vehicle for transportation, people minding guitars, support acts dropping in (Def Leppard no less. They were great), bodyguards trying to keep the crazy Irish Girl away (me!) The many hundreds of stagehands exhausted as they arrived back trudging into the bar (I like to people watch).

Earlier that day as Bon Jovi left for the gig I was confronted with a tall, bald, German 'don't f&@k with me' bodyguard who threatened to call security on me (I only wanted to peek into the basement car park) and was turned away. Not to be defeated and having had 3 days to suss things out - I went down to the car park this afternoon as the band left for Münich. After a few words, I was 'allowed' to stand aside and watch Bon Jovi (not JBJ) as they went at warp speed from the lift to their awaiting blackened out van.

I said "goodbye" they mumbled "bye" and off they went.

JBJ is like a ghost, he's in the wind, snapped his fingers and clicked his red heels together like Dorothy in the Wizard of Oz and vanished (I cried).

As I get ready to board Aer Lingus to go home. I am grateful for so much. Grateful I have a home to go back to with a loving, beautiful, supportive, kind, witty (he makes me laugh everyday) husband and the best dog ever, Toby where I am loved unconditionally, even though sometimes I'm irrational and my actions are spontaneous for want of a better word. I am grateful for my family and friends who encouraged me to go on this mad Bon Jovi adventure. As my wise older sister said –

"it's only when you're gone that you appreciate what you have at home."

True, very true. It may not have yielded ALL the results I had hoped for but look at what I did achieve!

I met my idols and had great chats with them, experienced a concert in a different country, met not so nice people BUT then, today I met a lovely

German couple who's hardships have put lots into perspective for me-thank you Beata and Oudo. I wish you both well.

Lastly, I am grateful to be able to put myself first. I wanted to push myself and truthfully, I did. I wanted to meet Bon Jovi - I achieved that dream. JBJ missed out on meeting me! One has to flip the negative to a positive. I feel like I had to put all of this in words, for myself mostly.

Going forward, I want to put it out there to be kind. It costs nothing. A kind gesture and/or word could make someone's day or change a life. I also want to be more supportive of others and practice what I preach on a daily basis in school- "follow your dreams!"

So what's next? Actually, a career break. Time out from school. Time where I can concentrate on the people and things I love, hopefully meet JBJ and time to dream more dreams....

I am a teacher and everyday I try to be kind and teach my students to be kind to each other. It is my wish to meet JBJ and to show people that dreams DO come true.

Why can't it be me???!!!"

Tracey Wade (Galway)

"They are always amazing.

Landsdowne Road, Dublin 2003, should have been my first but I mislaid my ticket two weeks before the gig. I turned the house upside down, but no luck. Three days after, I found it in a drawer I had checked several times.

Gutted.

*I can't get to other countries but I haven't missed an Irish one since. Punchestown was definitely awesome, and although '**Hallelujah**' isn't their own song, being in the crowd with phone lights swaying and thousands of voices singing gently was truly magical enough to bring me to tears."*

Dee Brown (Mayo, Ireland)

"Dublin 15th June 2019.

I love Bon Jovi and have done from day one.

I have three girls who all love the band and this year I was able to share the experience with my older two girls. They were embarrassed by my singing and dancing but who cares I was there to party and they soon joined in.

*The band put on the most amazing show with an unreal playlist with '**Captain Crash...**' and '**Amen**' being my favourites.*

Can't wait until Bon Jovi come back missing them already."

Kathryn Ruddell (Ireland)

Bounce

1) Undivided.....................3:53
2) Everyday.....................3:00
3) The Distance................4:48
4) Joey.........................4:54
5) Misunderstood..............3:30
6) All About Lovin' You.......3:46
7) Hook Me Up..................3:54
8) Right Side of Wrong........5:50
9) Love me Back to Life......4:09
10) You Had Me From Hello...3:49
11) Bounce.....................3:11
12) Open All Night.............4:22

Release Date: 8th October 2002
Producer: Luke Ebbin, Jon Bon Jovi, Richie Sambora, Desmond Child, Andreas Carlsson
Singles: 'Everyday', 'Misunderstood', 'All About Lovin' You', 'Bounce' 'The Distance'

"My Personal Favourite Album.
We had 'All About Lovin' You' for our first dance at our wedding!"
Michael Drew (Ireland)

"Bounce' - perhaps one the best 'rocking' albums, getting back to roots, still in a modern way, with some great thoughts as well.
And perhaps pointlessly the most undervalued album.
I can't forget the live broadcast from the Shepherd's Bush Empire, London, watching in a movie theatre in Budapest."
Balázs Márton (Budapest, Hungary)

"Bounce' album is better now, to me, than when it was new.
It holds up well, lyrically. Especially 'The Distance', 'Undivided' and 'Hook Me Up'! So three on one album - not bad at all, guys!"
Melissa Martin Collins (USA)

"Total class.
This album got me through a very difficult time in my life and inspired me to 'Bounce' back too. 'Love Me Back to Life' - absolutely brilliant song."
Julie Pinkney Hoyle (UK)

"Undivided' is an anthem for the raw anger we all felt on 9/11. It says everything that I wanted to say after that event. Beautifully done piece musically and emotionally. For me, it helps keep the memory of those affected by this tragedy alive."
Lynnette Staley (Carmi, Illinois, USA)

"First album I brought with my wages, played this album to death.
'Misunderstood', 'Everyday', 'All About Lovin' You', 'Undivided' and 'Bounce' - all have had their days as my ringtone at one point.
Perfect mix for me of rocking songs and power ballads one of my favourite albums by far."
Dario Briatore (Loughborough, UK)

*"We were driving through New Mexico last week and passed by the VLA (Very Large Array). Of course it reminded me of the '**Bounce**' album cover! One of the pics I took..."*
Kelly Van Dyke (USA)

"One of the most undervalued albums of all time but with great pieces."
Fabrizio Camporese (Milan, Italy)

"Great album to unite the world after 9/11. Some great rock tunes like 'Bounce' and 'Everyday'. But also some great ballads like 'All About Lovin' You' and 'You Had Me From Hello'.
Bon Jovi back to their rocking roots."
Robin 'Shakespeare' Grigsby (Teynham, UK)

"While touring in 2003 in support of 'Bounce', Bon Jovi taped a VH1 show called 'Command the Band'. That contest and reality TV show turned my dreams and love for this band into real life.
My family and I shared moments together with this amazing band that were solely because of their appreciation of their fans. They literally put me and then my daughter on top of the world.
The songs from 'Bounce' will forever remain the soundtrack from my experience of a lifetime.
My never ending thanks and undying love always to Bon Jovi."
Kathy Wilcox Rushforth (River Edge, New Jersey, USA)

KATHY WILCOX RUSHFORTH

"What guitars on this album!
Concept album - undervalued, with the only demerit of being released after 'Crush'!"
Alessandro Mosco (Italy)

*"Have loved the band since I first heard '**Bad Name...**' and was hooked. The first impression was 'wow that mans voice, that song' then – 'the whole band is amazing'.*
*The very first song I actually noticed guitar sound. Richie is simply awesome. But every time I here '**Bounce**' it makes me laugh our loud. Due to an interview I saw where Jon was wearing a T-shirt saying 'bounce on this'."*
Donna Brimson (Portsmouth, UK)

"Yeeee."
Yvonne Young (Cumbernauld, Scotland, UK)

"This is the very first Bon Jovi album I bought, back in 2003...
I had just graduated from high school, so for me it also represented independence, in some way.
I think it's so far their best album since their 'reunion' in 2000."
Elena Emanuela (Turin, Italy)

*"One of my favourite albums of Bon Jovi, I love '**The Distance**', '**Everyday**' and '**Bounce**' of course to name but a few..."*
Tanya Kennedy (In the World)

"One of my best albums."
Minna Garloz (Estado de México, Mexico)

*"Man, this album is really important with great Songs such as '**Undivided**', '**Everyday**', '**Hook Me Up**', '**The Distance**'... and a personal thought: I Lost my virginity while this album was playing LOL."*
Jefferson Mota (Santo André, Brazil)

"I loved this album, but this unfortunately started the 'Political democratic' Bon Jovi song writing that we are a custom to today.
I loved just about everything of Bon Jovi, but I didn't like how mostly he went all Political writing.
*My least favorite album is '**What About Now**'. It was just a weird album, just as weird as '**Burning Bridges**'. But I actually prefer '**Burning Bridges**' over because we can."*
Russell LoPresti (Jim Thorpe, Pennsylvania, USA)

"The very best album."
Adriano Margherita (Taranto, Italy)

"Bon Jovi is like opium - captivates and addicts."
Dieter Walentowski (Lutol Mokry, Poland)

*"**Bounce**', reminds me of my honeymoon trip. Listened to them songs, while we travelled in our car.*
Like Those songs our marriage still strong all these years gone by."
Claudio Lourenco Calado (La Chaux-de-Fonds, Switzerland)

"Songs of faith, as always, great pictures on back screen of fellow fire-fighters who gave it all on 9/11... God bless you all x."
Dave Axel Foley (UK)

"Good album."
Julie Tyson (UK)

"Luv this CD, this is the one that Jon let the fans have there say as to what the title of it woz gonna be!!"
Ashleigh Auld (Belfast)

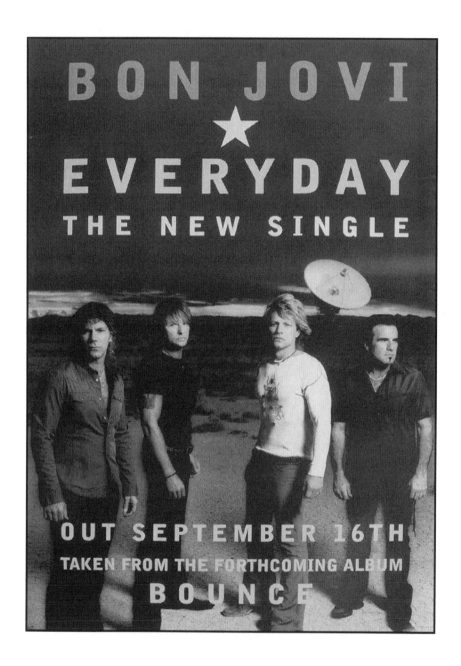

"Bon Jovi has been my favourite group for 35 years.
I first heard of them at rock nights that hubby and I went to when we first started dating. I would sit there every Friday and the DJ would play this one song every week 'shot through the heart' the dance floor would fill to capacity, I loved it! I had to have it...
*So I asked the DJ who it was and he showed me the album cover. With this knowledge I got myself on a train to Liverpool with my partner and trawled through the albums in HMV until I found it, but I found not just this Bon Jovi album but also '7800 **Fahrenheit**'.*
I was over the moon.
*From this point on I have never looked back. I fell in love with his voice; at the beginning I only had the picture on the album cover for ages to see how he looked. It was ages until '**Slippery...**' came out and I saw him for the first time performing on television. Since then I have every album etc. all kinds of stuff. Seen them live 14 times and still love them as much now."*

Alison Phelan (UK)

Luxembourg

(Including My Favourite Concert)

"Luxembourg, 11th of June 1996.
The first and still the only one Concert in our small Country.
The Concert was open air - sold out of course - with 35,000 people having so much fun, it was amazing.
The date was also special for me because it's my birthday, so I'm proud and glad to say that Bon Jovi played the only Concert in Luxembourg on that Day."
Guy Overmann (Dudelange)

Mexico

(Including My Favourite Concert)

*"**Because We Can**' tour - Mexico City."*
Patricia Casas (Mexico)

"1996 in Frankfurt Germany, at the Waldstadion.
19 songs plus 10 extras. The concert was amazing. Almost 3hrs long.
I will never ever forget it."
Kirstin Opfer (Mexico City, Mexico)

This Left Feels Right

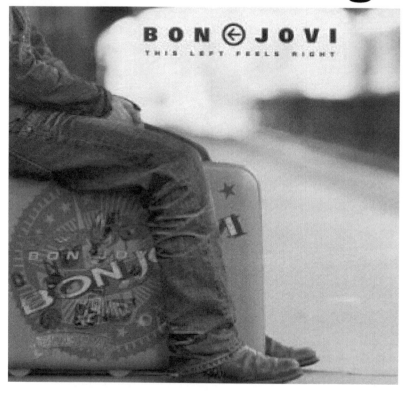

1) Wanted Dead or Alive...................3:43
2) Livin' on a Prayer ft. Olivia d'Abo........3:41
3) Bad Medicine.............................4:27
4) It's My Life..................................3:42
5) Lay Your Hands on Me....................4:27
6) You Give Love a Bad Name...............3:29
7) Bed of Roses.............................5:38
8) Everyday.....................................3:45
9) Born to Be My Baby......................5:27
10) Keep the Faith...........................4:12
11) I'll Be There for You.....................4:21
12) Always.......................................4:18

Release Date: 4th November 2003
Producer: Patrick Leonard, Jon Bon Jovi,
Richie Sambora
Singles: 'Wanted Dead or Alive', 'It's My Life', 'Always'

"Not sure how I feel about this one! A strange experience!"
Julie Pinkney Hoyle (UK)

*"Well, in the 'Live DVD' released alongside this album, at least we heard a little bit of preview of **Last Man Standing** because that's all I've got on this one.*
The DVD is better than the audio CD."
Melissa Martin Collins (USA)

*"**This Left Feels Right**' was a different way of hearing your favorite Bon Jovi songs. A good twist on their great hits."*
Pam Barrett (USA)

*"The stripped down version of '**It's My Life**' shows just how good the song is. It also shows how good Jon's voice is.*
I certainly wasn't blown away by the whole album, but some tracks were good. I would say it was an experiment that kind of worked."
Robin 'Shakespeare' Grigsby (Teynham, UK)

"I loved this album. My daughter gave me the DVD of the album, really, really brilliant vocal, loved all the slowed down versions, quite 'bluesy'."
April May (Saltford, UK)

"BEST GROUP EVER."
Kimberley Stuart (In the World)

"Love it! One of my faves!"
Deborah Cox (UK)

*"**This Left Feels Right**' is the first DVD I bought.*
It was from the Borgata Casino and Jon performed every song in a slow sexy way. My sister and I both fell in love with him as soon as we watched it. We became fans and then attended 13 concerts... I love JBJ."
Shirley Morrow Rishell (Kunkletown, Pennsylvania, USA)

"Some fans loved it, others hated it. I loved it as it showed the band being adventurous.
*The piano driven version of '**It's My Life**' on here is better than the original in my opinion.*
They did 2 shows at the Borgata in Atlantic City to record the DVD and they were 2 of the best Jovi shows I've been to."
Michael Dewsnap (UK)

"I have this DVD as well.
I don't turn the volume up quite as loud with this one!"
Janet Luce (The Pas, Manitoba, Canada)

"This is my most album!!
I love the new spin they put on already great songs!!!"
Becky Taylor (Scottville, Michigan, USA)

*"I had to include a Bon Jovi song on our wedding day, so our first dance was to '**Living On a Prayer**' from this album."*
Carrie Burke (Manchester, UK)

"The first track of the album was mind blowing... you can keep listening on and on and on."
Anuja Gupta (Gauhati, India)

"Helen Black u luv this album. I have played it constantly in my car with memories of u not only knowing n belting out every word. But I pretend to harmonize wi ya lol."
Tanya Brown (Newtonards, Northern Ireland, UK)

"This album has a lot of memories for me.
*My hubby is not a fan, but when we were going through a bad patch he rang me up one day and played '**I'll Be There for You**' and '**Always**'.*
1st time he showed his soft side.
We celebrated 25 years this year. I love the whole album."
Lynne Foley (Middlesbrough, UK)

"Not my favorite album."
Shari Morales (Kenosha, Wisconsin, USA)

"Didn't know what to think of the album and was leaning towards not liking it, but after the shows I felt a new sort of respect for what they did with the songs."
Miriam de Jong (Netherlands)

"I have it and I love it super!!!"
Ana Diaz (Mexicali, Baja, California, USA)

"I was a finalist in a contest to win 2 tix to the TLFR concert @ Borgata, but another girl won.
I posted on the message boards that she had won the tix. I had never met this girl before, but as fate would have it, she ended up taking me to the concert with her and she let me stay at her house in Brigantine overnight. Gina and I are still very good friends 16 years later.
BJ has introduced me to many lifelong friends through our mutual like of the band.
My Jovi friends Diane, Nancy & Shirley and I all still keep in touch to this day. Thanks to Diane, I got to attend the 'RRHOF' induction, too. Those bonds we all formed are priceless."
Sherri Johnson Riddle (USA)

SHERRI JOHNSON RIDDLE

"I was one who loved this.
And at the Borgata I especially loved 'You Give Love A Bad Name', I've never seen Jon be as sexy as this was. Whew!
And Sherri, I couldn't agree more about all the friendships we have made."
Nanci Rossman (Glen Burnie, Maryland, USA)

NANCY ROSSMAN

Netherlands

(Including My Favourite Concert)

"July, Nijmegen it was all great because it was a great show.
Julie Tactor (Sprang-Capella, Netherlands)

"My love band."
Sabina Gaskin (Lutjebroke, Netherlands)

"13 June 2019 Goffertpark, Nijmegen."
Steffanie Bos (Netherlands)

New Zealand

(Including My Favourite Concert)
"Where There is a Will, There is a Way"
By Becks Hart

*"In life there are many people that play a part in the making of the person you are today. For me, Bon Jovi has played a major role over the last 33 years through their music and their selfless down to earth attitude. I first heard of Bon Jovi in 1986 with the release of '**Slippery When Wet**' when it hit the airwaves in New Zealand. At that time I had just reached my teenage years, and was about to start High School, soon to be a little fish in a big pond. I grew up in a relatively small town in North Canterbury where everybody knew everybody, and was the middle child with an older sister and a younger brother. It's true what they say about the middle child. I had always felt in some instances exclusion and, in retaliation behaviour wise, would act out just to get attention. I wanted to stand out. I was always a determined and strong willed girl, would give anything a go, good or bad and had a tendency to shoot my mouth off and think of the consequences later.*

*With the release of '**Slippery…**' it was just what I needed at that time in my life, I was going through puberty, emotional and trying to fit in. '**Living on a Prayer**' was the song that gave me the Bon Jovi bug, from then I was hooked. I can recall many hours just sitting on the floor* *watching the video over and over again, pausing on my favourite part, where Jon shakes his booty 3 times, and replaying it.*

I was working part time and any money that I had would be spent on Bon Jovi paraphernalia. I would often buy magazines and read what fans would do to meet their idols. Hence this is where the idea came up to write the word 'Please' in hope that Bon Jovi would come to New Zealand. I have always believed where there is a will there is a way.

The crusade of writing pleases had begun. I would take my notebooks to school and my friends and I would write 'pleases' at every opportunity we could muster. I recall getting busted writing them in science class and having them taken off me, and being told I could have them back at the end of school. This I was not happy about, and after a few choice words was removed from class and sent to the principal's office. I earnt a week long detention but at least my notebook was returned to me.

Writing the 'pleases' continued over the next year with the aid of my friends and even their parents stepped in and wrote some also. Finally I heard the news that Bon Jovi was going to be visiting New Zealand with only one show in Auckland on November 18th 1989. Auckland is in the North Island and I lived in the South Island. I was ecstatic, my dream had come true, Bon Jovi was coming to New Zealand. My next plan of attack was what to do now with all my 'pleases'. Then an opportunity arose when I heard that Ms. Sue White from 91ZMFM, which was one of our local radio stations, was going to be in Kaiapoi, my hometown, at the local Rugby Club for the Gala Day. This is where my plan started to unfold. I loaded up my backpack with all my 'pleases' that we had to date.

I had one exercise book that held 25,000 "pleases", notebooks with varying amounts and a folder. In total I had 112,382 "pleases". I also had photos of my room which was covered in posters including the ceiling. Sue appeared very impressed and said she would love to come around and see my room, which she did at a later date and also met my Mum and Dad. I explained to her why I wrote the 'pleases' and that I would love to meet Bon Jovi as I was their biggest fan in Kaiapoi.

I had many phone calls with Sue while she was on air as she had given me the private line to ring her on, she probably thought I was the biggest pain in the arse but at that time I was a headstrong, emotional teenager on a mission.   Unbeknown to me, Sue had been working behind the scenes with her manager and the Frontier Touring Company who were promoting the tour, and having secret phone calls to Mum and Dad.

I remember Dad saying to me "Rebecca, come here we would like to talk to you."
Inside I'm thinking "oh shit, what have I done, another phone call from the school about my behaviour?" The only time I would get called Rebecca was if I was in trouble.

Dad said to me "Have you been good, are you going to keep on being good?"
I replied "Yes." With a puzzled, confused look on my face.

He then says "How would you like to go and see Bon Jovi?"

I said "Fuck yes" and started crying. Dad then said "you can go, but only if Sharleen will take you." Sharleen is my cousin who lives in Auckland. He kept on talking but I didn't hear what was said as I was in a state of shock and bewilderment. The realisation had yet to set in; I was going to see Bon Jovi in Auckland.
Then Mum says to Dad "Aren't you going to tell her the rest?"
I said "What do you mean? I haven't got a backstage pass, have I?" ever so hopeful.
He says "No." my heart sank but at least on the positive side I was going to the Bon Jovi show, I would see my idols. He continued "You have two."
Well that set the tears flowing like a river. I was going to meet Bon Jovi, holy shit, that would be a dream come true. I was absolutely dumbfounded and blown away. Then it dawned on me, the 'pleases' had worked, all 112,382 of them.

Once I had calmed down I started ringing my friends to let them know that I was going to Bon Jovi and had 2 backstage passes. I was going to meet the Jersey Boys! I thanked them profusely for their help with writing the 'pleases', they were just so happy that it had worked. The next day at school word got around, I felt like a celebrity, even some of the teachers came and congratulated me. I rang Sue to thank her so much for what she had done for me and the strings she had pulled. She came home to hand deliver the two concert tickets and a letter to show where we were to pick up the back stage passes.
It was the morning of the concert, I barely had any sleep at all, I was too excited 'Today' was the day. I had an appointment at the hairdressers to get my hair done, packed up the t-shirt Mum had printed for me, so I

*could get it signed and the '**New Jersey**' project to give them all as a gift.*

Once in Auckland we headed to the Hyatt Regency where I was to collect the passes, on opening the envelope I discovered 2 more concert tickets. We tried and tried continuously to contact Sharleen's brother but the line was engaged. Then I came up with the idea to ring the phone company and asked if they were able to cut into the phone call as I had fallen off my bike and needed help. This was an obvious lie but it worked and we spoke with Aaron and offered him and his girlfriend the extra tickets. By then it was about 4.30pm, in 30 minutes we had to be at the side gate to be admitted into the backstage area.

I was so excited but also quiet knowing that within a short time I would be face to face with my rock idols. We were let through to the meet and greet area; I was shaking, trembling with anticipation. Then I bent down and underneath the tent I could see their legs. OMG the Jersey Boys were less than 15 metres away. The tears started, then as they got closer the more I cried, tears of joy, of course. I didn't want to cry but I couldn't help myself. Jon gave me a hug and told me not to cry, my legs felt like jelly, then Tico gave me a hug, soon followed by David. I was speechless, overwhelmed, looking back in hindsight I was a crying muppet. It is indescribable what meeting them meant and how down to earth and genuine they are. My tears dried up after the initial meeting which was good as I was able to speak with them all and have a conversation with each of them that wasn't unintelligible, and get photos without the tears.

*The concert was amazing '**Lay Your Hands On Me**' was the first song they played and sung. It felt like there was no tomorrow, word for word, still wanting to pinch myself as I couldn't believe I had met them and was now rocking out to their songs. It just goes to show that if you put your mind to something you want, where there's a will there's a way.*

On Saturday November 18th, 1989 my dream came true.
This would not have been achieved without the support and help of my friends, Sue White and of course Mum and Dad for letting me go. Bon Jovi was my first concert and along with many photographs I kept my t-shirt, a treasured memory from that time. My eldest son wore it many years later when I took him and his brother to their first rock concert, Bon Jovi of course."
Rebecca Hart (Kaiapoi, New Zealand)

100,000,000
Bon Jovi Fans Can't Be Wrong

1) Why Aren't You Dead?...................................3:31
2) The Radio Saved My Life Tonight...............5:08
3) Taking It Back....................................4:17
4) Someday I'll Be Saturday Night...............5:18
5) Miss Fourth of July.............................5:40
6) Open All Night (#2).............................5:47
7) These Arms Are Open All Night................5:20
8) I Get A Rush.....................................2:57
9) Someday Just Might Be Tonight...............4:13
10) Thief of Hearts................................4:17
11) Last Man Standing.............................4:32
12) I Just Want to Be Your Man....................3:28
13) Garageland......................................3:26
14) Starting All Over Again........................3:44
15) Maybe Someday.................................4:43
16) Last Chance Train.............................4:31
17) The Fire Inside.................................4:50

18) Every Beat of My Heart........................4:49
19) Rich Man Living in a Poor Man's House.....4:22
20) The One That Got Away........................4:48
21) You Can Sleep While I Dream................4:53
22) Outlaws of Love................................3:20
23) Good Guys Don't Always Wear White........4:29
24) We Rule the Night..............................4:09
25) Edge of a Broken Heart......................4:36
26) Sympathy......................................5:23
27) Only in My Dreams............................5:07
28) Shut Up and Kiss Me..........................2:47
29) Crazy Love....................................4:25
30) Lonely at the Top..............................3:51
31) Ordinary People..............................4:07
32) Flesh and Bone................................5:01
33) Satellite......................................4:56
34) If I Can't Have Your Love....................4:15
35) Real Life......................................3:52
36) Memphis Lives in Me..........................3:03
37) Too Much of a Good Thing....................4:23
38) Love Ain't Nothing But a Four Letter Word..4:14
39) Love Ain't Nothing But a Four Letter Word..4:08
40) River Runs Dry................................3:57
41) Always..5:46
42) Kidnap an Angel..............................5:56
43) Breathe..3:40
44) Out of Bounds................................3:46
45) Letter to a Friend............................4:19
46) Temptation....................................4:23
47) Gotta Have a Reason..........................4:59
48) All I Wanna Do Is You........................3:03
49) Billy..4:32
50) Nobody's Hero................................4:33
51) Livin' on a Prayer............................3:52

Release Date: 16th November 2004
Producer: Patrick Leonard, Andy Johns, Jon Bon Jovi,
Richie Sambora, Obie O'Brien
Singles: 'The Radio Saved My Life Tonight'

"I love the unreleased tracks."
Daniel Spera (Brazil)

"Yesterday, today, tomorrow and always, Bon Jovi."
Nuria Nuria (Spain)

"Waited with anticipation for this box set! **'The Radio Saved My Life Tonight'**.
PS: I could have gone without those golden suits though!"
Melissa Martin Collins (USA)

"From another JERSEY GIRL.
YOUR MUSIC MAKES ME FEEL WONDERFUL.
I have this album. And all others."
Katharine Dudek (Merrimac, Massachusetts, USA)

"Have it."
Lois Jeanine Bush Fahrney (Elyria, Ohio, USA)

"I HAVE THAT & Loving all the Golden songs on it."
Kristen Saffian (USA)

"All I kept thinking was –
"It's about time JBJ opened up the vault and shared some gems with us fans!!"
Lori Mascola Broslovsky (Carlstadt, New Jersey, USA)

"I love all the songs on here, songs never been released, my amazing hubby bought it me as 1 of my Christmas surprises.
U know wot tunes woz playing all Christmas & New Year's."
Jasmine Morgan (UK)

"The boys released this as a birthday gift to me and celebrated with gold suits.
In all seriousness, so precious to hear the makings of a lifetime of songs that I hung on every word to and songs I never heard before.
*"**Open All Night**" CD 1 Track 6 has been played so many times I'm surprised the CD still plays.'*
Tanya Regan (Australia)

"Gracias."
Liliana Barajas (Brazil)

"*Those CD's sucked.*"
Lisa Pizon Waddell (Schaumburg, Illinois, USA)

"*It is a good box set. I like '**The Radio Saved My Life Tonight**', but all the Bon Jovi songs take me back to a period in my life.*"
Jeremie Ferrel (Russellville, Arkansas, USA)

"*It's the best.*"
Kristen Saffian (USA)

"*Got it.*"
Karen Lebiedzinski (South Bend, Indiana, USA)

"*Love this box set.
I have 3 - one for the car, one for upstairs and one for downstairs; don't like the gold suits, but that has nothing to do with music lol.*"
Madeline Steer (Habrough, UK)

"Love this box-set.
It is my go-to music on road trips.
So many great songs that had never been released. A special gift for fans.
Great presentation with the booklet and the DVD."
Margaret Farr (Brampton, Ontario, Canada)

"My pride 'n' joy I saved up for weeks for this one it cost me £59."
Rose Milne (Aberdeen)

Norway

"Been a fan since 1986 and still love them. Love all the songs on their albums."
Åse-Marit Nerring (Odnes, Norway)

Have a Nice Day

1) Have a Nice Day.................................3:48
2) I Want to Be Loved.............................3:49
3) Welcome to Wherever You Are...............3:47
4) Who Says You Can't Go Home..................4:40
5) Last Man Standing.............................4:37
6) Bells of Freedom..............................4:55
7) Wildflower.....................................4:13
8) Last Cigarette.................................3:38
9) I Am...3:53
10) Complicated...................................3:37
11) Novocaine.....................................4:49
12) Story of My Life..............................4:08
13) Who Says You Can't Go Home (Duet)........3:50

Release Date: 20th September 2005

Producer: John Shanks, Jon Bon Jovi, Richie Sambora, Rick Parasher, Dann Huff, Desmond Child

Singles: 'Have a Nice Day', 'I Want to Be Loved', 'Who Says You Can't Go Home', 'Welcome to Wherever You Are'

"Great album."
Yvonne Young (Cumbernauld, Scotland, UK)

"I have this song as my ring tone. I remember seeing the song on TV when it first came out. Absolutely love it.
When in concert Jon sings it it's such a happy song it brings smiles on faces."
Michelle Donnelly (Port Macquarie, New South Wales, Australia)

"How I feel every single day."
Jennifer Woods King (USA)

"I went to the 'Have a Nice Day' concert in Dublin, it was my 1st ever Bon Jovi concert and I loved it."
Pamela Halliday (Carrickfergus, Northern Ireland, UK)

"Have a Nice Day'... what a song!
The message behind it really spoke to me, when life starts to gets to you, don't take things to heart, stand up and give life the finger.
I had the have a nice day face tattooed on my arm to remind me everyday to be strong."
Dario Briatore (Loughborough, UK)

"Have a Nice Day'."
Tristan Gomola (Clarence, Pennsylvania, USA)

"I remember being super excited about this album, and this tour!
It gave us the rocked up version of 'Last Man Standing' and it's the tour we were able to visit and see the band in New Jersey!"
Melissa Martin Collins (USA)

"Up there with with 'New Jersey' in my book."
Eddie Bland (Cannock, UK)

"Loved this one as soon as it came out. So many inspirational songs to keep strong. My go to album when I need uplifting."
Sarah Miles (Linford, Essex, UK)

"THIS is my favourite album!
I love the music I love the Smirk!
When I listen to this album, I hear the bad ass and the soft part of this band! Kind of like me!!!"
Diane Courchesne (Canada)

"My fave album! Know every word to every song."
Georgina Cantlon (Hamilton, Ontario, Canada)

"So many amazing songs and lyrics that really resonate - so much so I had some of them tattooed!
An album that is so easy to relate to and kick ass to listen to!"
Lauren Fay Smith (UK)

"That must be the evil Mr Cool Ade."
Johnny Tusa (New York, New York, USA)

"I've been listening to Bon Jovi since 1983 when my 2nd son was born. This is one of my favorite albums.
When I first listened to this album, I could not believe what I was hearing! I was at a low point in my life when I was down and out and every song on this album spoke to me.
It helped me turn my life around! I started "Having a Nice Day".
Deborah DeVito-DiGregorio (North Babylon, New York, USA)

"Bon Jovi, Poet from the soul."
Danie Gaudreau (Montreal, Quebec, Canada)

"My Favorite song, I listen to it every day on my way to work.
It's also my ringtone."
Doris LaVolpa (USA)

"I love this Album I have a hat with **'Have A Nice Day'** *on it."*
Lena Farrell (Sydney, Nova Scotia, Canada)

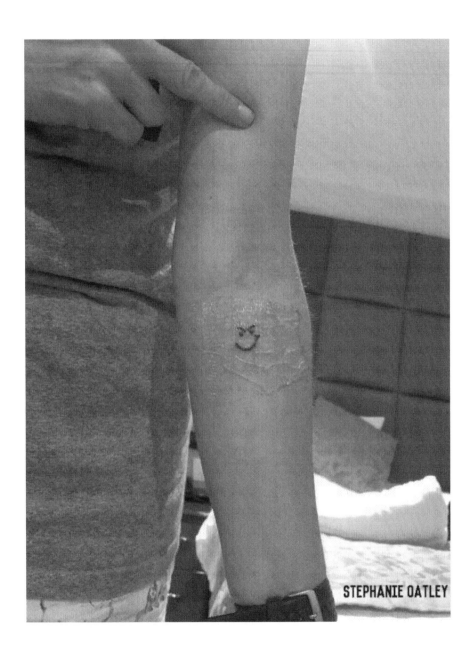

Paraguay

(Including My Favourite Concert)

"Live from London - the best of all."
Miguel Angel (Luque, Paraguay)

Lost Highway

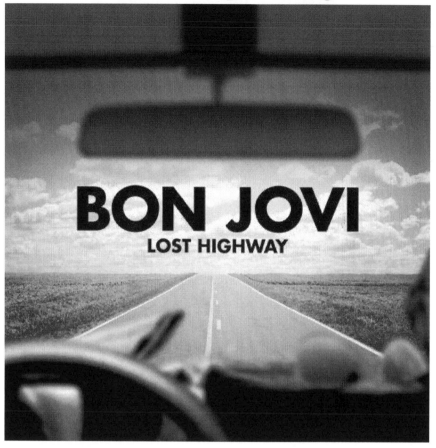

Release Date: 8th June 2007
Producer: Dann Huff, John Shanks, Desmond Child
Singles: '(You Want To) Make a Memory,
                 'Lost Highway', 'Whole Lot of Leavin'
                 'Till We Ain't Strangers Anymore',
                 'Summertime',

"This is one of my all time favorite albums.
My husband and I and our best friends took a road trip that summer from Michigan to see them in Wyoming, an eventful 18-hour drive to say the least!
We survived a flat tire and tornado warnings to get there and waited in line for general admission tickets with cows in pens next to us, no joke!
Here's me and my bestie Yvette Shockey that day in July 2007."
Anna Galloro Shafto (Commerce, Michigan, USA)

"Seriously a life-changing, memory-making experience!"
Yvette Shockey (Michigan, USA)

*"**Lost Highway**'... if I am totally honest not a fan.*
*Sounds strange because there's a few tracks I did like on there but I just felt that they'd lost that "Bon Jovi edge" that I'd come to know and love. The title track gave me the feeling of life on the road a little, '**Till We Ain't Strangers Anymore**' was on every time my then girlfriend and I just wanted to chill out listening to music and '**(You Want To) Make a Memory**' was the song I chose to learn on guitar to play for my sisters wedding... but then she didn't get married, still was worth my learning because I still play to this day."*
Dario Briatore (Loughborough, UK)

"Brilliant album."
Julie Tyson (UK)

"This is one of my faves."
Julie Marsden (UK)

"This is another great album of Bon Jovi! I wore this CD out. I love it!!"
Deborah DeVito-DiGregorio (North Babylon, New York, USA)

"Brilliant! Fun! Love it."
Julie Pinkney Hoyle (UK)

"I absolutely love this album...
Absolutely love the country vibe. Its fun, full of great lyrics and although it's not their usual style... It's still got that Bon Jovi feel through and through....with the added bonus of violinist."
Jess Cussen Stevens (UK)

"We got it going on..."
Clare Quee (Sydney, Australia)

"Love this album!!! Definitely feels like summertime!!"
Becky Taylor (Scottville, Michigan, USA)

"One of my favorite albums, listen to it very often.
Beautiful songs, beautiful lyrics and music. So love my Bon Jovi music!"
Brenda Merritt Stotts (Joshua, Texas, USA)

"Love this CD!"
Jackie Pintaric (Australia)

"One of my faves when I am on a long car journey.
Loads of songs to get you singing loud and tapping your feet!!"
Sarah Miles (Linford, Essex, UK)

*"Oh gosh I love this album, '**Make a Memory**' is one of my favourite tracks of all time."*
April May (Saltford, UK)

"Awesome album!"
Georgina Cantlon (Hamilton, Ontario, Canada)

*"The beginning of the end, every album after '**Have a Nice Day**' has got progressively worse, to the extent I haven't seen them live since the '**Have a Nice Day**' tour."*
John Darren Halliday (Chorley, UK)

"I always remember getting into trouble in high school; the head teacher called my mum and looked puzzled waiting for her to answer, saying, "Is there supposed to be music playing?"
*I replied "yeah- it's '**Something like Summertime**'!"*
For this and so many other reasons, this album makes me smile!"
Lauren Fay Smith (UK)

"Love love this album!!!
This album/tour gave me lots of new friends that have become quite close and still share adventures to this day!!!
One of my favourite album for road (toad) trips!!!"
Diane Courchesne (Canada)

Philippines

(Including My Favourite Concert)

"My favorite band ever..."
Adiar Ed'n (Philippines)

*"**Crush**' tour at Zurich, Switzerland."*
Christian Kent dela Torre (Philippines)

"My husband is a great fan of Jon bon Jovi!
*He loves to sing 'Dry County', 'Blaze of Glory' and a lot more of Bon Jovi's greatest songs... To meet his idol in person and have a duet is just like hitting the jackpot in lottery! '**Runaway**'... he can sing that song like Jon Bon Jovi."*
Lyn-iel Mequin (Urdaneta)

The Circle

1) We Weren't Born to Follow...........4:03
2) When We Were Beautiful.............5:18
3) Work for the Working Man...........4:04
4) Superman Tonight.....................5:12
5) Bullet...................................3:50
6) Thorn in My Side.....................4:05
7) Live Before You Die..................4:17
8) Brokenpromiseland..................4:57
9) Love's the Only Rule................4:38
10) Fast Cars............................3:16
11) Happy Now...........................4:21
12) Learn to Love........................4:39

Release Date: 10ᵗʰ November 2009
Producer: **John Shanks, Jon Bon Jovi, Richie Sambora**
Singles: **'We Weren't Born to Follow,**
            'Superman Tonight',
            'When We Were Beautiful',
            'Work for the Working Man (promo)'

*"**The Circle**'... the album that put my faith back in Bon Jovi after '**Lost Highway**'.*
*Kicking off with '**We Weren't Born to Follow**' I felt like this was the Bon Jovi I knew and loved, they were back and they were bringing a new message.*
*With songs like '**Work for the Working Man**', '**Live Before You Die**' and '**Happy Now**' I found myself on a whole new spiritual plain with a new lease for life.*
One of my fondest memories was travelling to London and seeing them preform on top of the Millennium Dome back in 2010, once again an amazing album and great concert."
Dario Briatore (Loughborough, UK)

*"One of '**the Circle**' Tours Concerts, I happened to see them on my Birthday and it was the best present ever to have gotten."*
Caryn Hurd (Camdenton, Missouri, USA)

"Good album."
Julie Tyson (UK)

"I would put this CD on love it, but I would cry like 'please, please let me go to this show' so I took my whole pay check got 2 tickets Louisville ky. I'll never forget it, got there they said that the seats I got they had a big light thing in the way so they moved us up but it wasn't front row nor backstage pass but I was there singing ever word to every song love JBJ forever."
Lucy N Donnie Terry (USA)

"Love it."
Yvonne Young (Cumbernauld, UK)

"Wow! Can't believe it's already been 10 years!
Seen 'the Circle' tour in Houston Texas with tickets that I won over a
radio station. I was SO EXCITED when I won them.
This was one of the show's where Phil X filled in for Richie."
Regina Duren (Humble, Texas, USA)

"I just would like to thank BJ for keeping me feeling young...
(71 years old)."
Katharine Dudek (Merrimac, Massachusetts, USA)

"Second 'the best' Bon Jovi album in my opinion."
Maja Szkudlínska (Łódź, Poland)

"I would love to see Jon Bob Jovi. I have been a fan since his
beginning!!!"
Donna Futscher (Melbourne, Kentucky, USA)

"I love this album - the concert was off-the-hook!
Bon Jovi puts on the best shows."
Deborah DiVito-DiGregorio (North Babylon, New York, USA)

"This album has one of my favorite songs on it
'When We Were Beautiful' love that song."
Carol McComsey Dailey (USA)

"This album has one of my favorite songs on it 'When We Were
Beautiful' - love that song."
Carol McComsey Dailey (USA)

Poland

"Will be in Warsaw July 12th, I'll be there."
Jolanta Tomczak (Białystok, Poland)

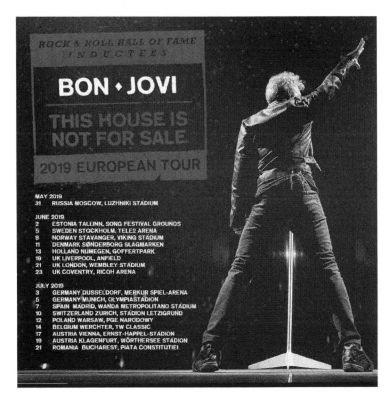

Greatest Hits

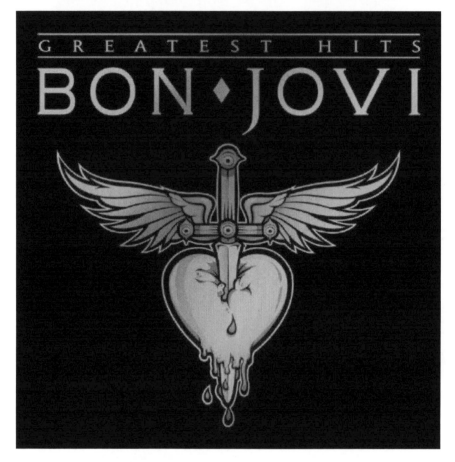

1) Livin' on a Prayer.........................4:13
2) You Give Love a Bad Name...............3:46
3) It's My Life.................................3:44
4) Have a Nice Day..........................3:48
5) Wanted Dead or Alive....................5:11
6) Bad Medicine.............................5:16
7) We Weren't Born to Follow..............4:03
8) I'll Be There for You.....................5:46
9) Born to Be My Baby......................4:40
10) Bed of Roses.............................6:38

11) Who Says You Can't Go Home............4:41
12) Lay Your Hands on Me....................3:49
13) Always....................................5:56
14) In These Arms............................5:19
15) What Do You Got.........................3:47
16) No Apologies.............................3:44
17) Runaway...................................3:53
18) Someday I'll Be Saturday Night.........4:39
19) Lost Highway.............................4:04
20) I'll Sleep When I'm Dead...............4:41
21) In and Out of Love.....................4:26
22) Keep the Faith...........................5:43
23) When We Were Beautiful...............5:17
24) Blaze of Glory...........................5:39
25) This Ain't a Love Song.................5:05
26) These Days...............................6:27
27) (You Want To) Make a Memory.........4:37
28) Blood on Blood..........................6:16
29) This Is Love, This Is Life.................3:25
30) The More Things Change...............3:53
31) This Is Our House (iTunes Bonus)......4:22

Release Date: 29ᵗʰ October 2010

Producer:	**Howard Benson, Tony Bongiovi, Jon Bon Jovi, Richie Sambora, Peter Collins, Luke Ebbin, Bruce Fairbairn, Danny Kortchmar, Lance Quinn, Bob Rock, John Shanks**
Singles:	**'What Do You Got?', 'No Apologies', 'This Is Our House'**

*"This is one of my favorite Bon Jovi CD's, I own all of them.
Took the picture of heart, dagger and wings and have it tattooed on my back."*
Michelle Newton (Penn Yan, New York, USA)

"Love that."
Monalisa Hughes (Canada)

"I also have this CD, all I can say is when I put any Bon Jovi song on I smile, then I want to cry because all my life since they came out I wanted to be a lucky one to meet Jon Bon Jovi - just love them him so much!"
Lucy N Donnie Terry (USA)

"Love this album."
Fawn Columbus (Morgan, Minnesota, USA)

"Omg, I love this album!! I listen to it all the time!!"
Mary Zilg Reinhard (USA)

"I didn't know what to think when I heard that Bon Jovi were releasing a second 'Greatest Hits' album.
I was partially worried that this was it for the guys, when bands start releasing greatest hits albums it's normally a sign that they are slowing down or retiring, thankfully this wasn't the case.
The better name for the album has to be 'the ultimate collection'. It was a joy to have all the 'fan favourites' on one CD and even better were the 4 brand new songs, my personal favourite being 'What Do You Got?'."
Dario Briatore (Loughborough, UK)

"Love this album. Have all the Bon Jovi albums, but my favourites are 'These Days' and 'Lost Highway' always listening to them."
Gill Carradice Trotzko (Wigan, UK)

"I was given this album as a Christmas gift by my son, I love it.
I have everything Bon Jovi ever came out with, I am a huge fan of his."
Lena Farrell (Sydney, Nova Scotia, Canada)

"Love this album as it has so many hits on it. Play it almost daily or 'This House Is Not For Sale' album."
Karen Mottau (Melbourne, Australia)

"I love the whole album it's my life."
Carol McComsey Dailey (USA)

Romania

(Including My Favourite Concert)

*"It all started back in the '90s when I saw Jon in the video of '**Blaze of Glory**' I was pretty young back then... My heart and ears started pounding –*

*"That's the one", I said to myself, my music ,my rock star ,that was '**Born to Be My Baby**'.*

Ever since Bon Jovi was in my heart, I grew up and grow old with them! They were always with me.

*When I first went to New York, Bon Jovi welcomed me with the launching of the '**Have a Nice Day**' album at Nokia Theatre.... On my wedding day with "Thank you for loving me", on the day my daughter was born, whenever I was happy or sad!*

They were part of my life and my family! I had a few wonderful Bon Jovi experiences in New York, New Jersey, Connecticut, Stuttgart and Bucharest. I was lucky to be close enough to interact with Jon as he is still charming today as he was 18 years ago!

Thank you for being my wings when I could fly and being my eyes when I couldn't see!

I will always love you!"

Luana BN (Romania)

*"The one in Romania 2019 tour: **'This House Is Not for Sale'**."*
Maria Costica (Bucharest)

"21st of July 2019, Bucharest, even if Jon was tired, we've seen him live,
that's what mattered most! Love him, anyway and the band, too!
Sambora was wrong to leave, all of them suffered, including Richie!
But, the show must go on!
We hope to see him in another country, if not in Romania!
'Slippery When Wet'.
Waiting for him in Bucharest!"
Mirela-Ana Voicu (Constanta, Romania)

Inside Out

1) Blood on Blood.....................6:18
2) Lost Highway.......................4:12
3) Born to Be My Baby................5:22
4) You Give Love a Bad Name........3:49
5) Whole Lot of Leavin'..............4:40
6) Raise Your Hands.................4:58
7) We Got It Going On................4:52
8) Have a Nice Day...................4:05
9) It's My Life.........................4:02
10) I'll Be There for You..............7:18
11) We Weren't Born to Follow........4:12
12) Wanted Dead or Alive.............5:38
13) Livin' on a Prayer.................6:18
14) Keep the Faith.....................7:09

Release Date: 27ᵗʰ November 2012
Producer: Bon Jovi, Richie Sambora, John Shanks
Desmond Child
Singles: None

"My daughter and I went to see this. We totally enjoyed it."
Denise McKinley (North Myrtle Beach, South Carolina, USA)

"I had a special viewing in Tupelo, Ms - only person in the theatre lol!"
Jennifer Woods King (Mississippi, USA)

"You rock Jon."
Yvonne Young (Cumbernauld, UK)

"Very sexy, sweet Jon."
Cheri Mathes (Wedt Saint Paul, Minnesota, USA)

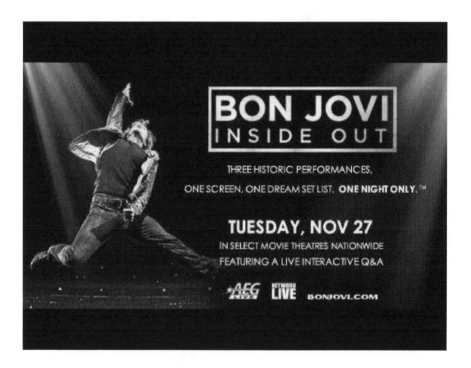

Slovenia

"Always been and will be my favorite band.
Been a fan since high-school ('95), where I met my love, who was also a fan.
We have been together ever since.
We first went to their concert in 2000 and again this year (2019)... And we both felt like we were 20 all over again.
We will surely be going to their concerts again and again...
'You Had Me From Hello'."
Nina Klemen (Kamnik, Slovenia)

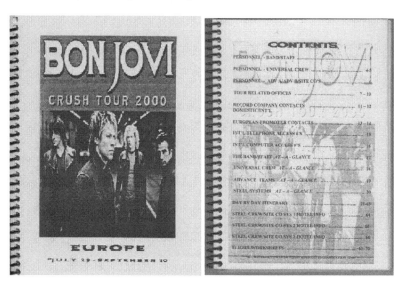

"Austria-Klagenfurt 2019. Tour: ***'This House Is Not for Sale'.***
It was amazing. Love Bon Jovi."
Klara Hrastovec (Vransko)

What About Now

1) Because We Can...........................4:00
2) I'm With You..............................3:44
3) What About Now.........................3:45
4) Pictures of You...........................3:58
5) Amen.......................................4:13
6) That's What the Water Made Me........4:26
7) What's Left of Me.........................4:35
8) Army of One...............................4:35
9) Thick as Thieves..........................4:58
10) Beautiful World..........................3:49
11) Room at the End of the World...........5:03
12) The Fighter...............................4:37

Release Date: 8th March 2013
Producer: John Shanks, Jon Bon Jovi, Rich Sambora
Singles: 'Because We Can', 'What About Now'

"My go to album when I'm driving and I'm getting tired. Instant foot thumping and loud singing!!"
Sarah Miles (Linford, Essex, UK)

"Been listening to this Album the last week, its a fantastic listen absolutely love it, its my fav at the mo.
Was remembering back in 2013 when we went to see Bon Jovi at Sunderland he sang one of my favs off the Album 'What's Left of Me', when the song finished there was the tiniest lull so I just shouted at the top of my voice, 'I'LL HAVE WHATS LEFT OF YOU JON', you can say I gave some around me a bit of a fright Ha."
Joyce Maddick (Newcastle-upon-Tyne, UK)

"What About Now'... an album that has mixed feelings for me.
The first track 'Because We Can' I will admit didn't quite have that Bon Jovi feel, it almost seemed a little 'watered down' from the guys but I am not one to turn my back on a Bon jovi album so I persevered and glad I did as I was pleasantly surprised at a few hidden gems.
My absolute favourite song has to be 'I'm With You", hearing this live with the crowd singing along was almost haunting, sending chills down my spine.
The ballads 'Old Habits Die Hard' and 'Not Running Anymore' (on the Japanese release) I could really connect with and I loved that we got a Ritchie song on the album...even though he's no longer in the band truly 'Every Road Leads Home to You' brother (Japan release)."
Dario Briatore (Loughborough, UK)

"It's ok. It's actually my least favorite.
I get weird vibes from this album and 'Burning Bridges'. I think I feel some of the songs don't make sense to me, and I think it screams too politically correct.
My three favorites are 'Because We Can', 'I'm With You' and 'Water..."
Russell LoPresti (Jim Thorpe, Pennsylvania, USA)

"It was at Villa Park England - my daughter took me for birthday."
Carl Antony Bellamy (UK)

"Familiar voice and style."
Georgina Cantlon (Hamilton, Ontario, Canada)

*"**What About Now'** — the album whose tour saw the departure of Sambora. So it's a good album, but Sambora leaving is how I remember this album."*
Melissa Martin Collins (USA)

"Love this album, but there again I love them all.
Listened to it every day coming home from work on the bus."
Donna Watson (UK)

"Great album. Some great songs on it. Very mature album also.
*Love '**Pictures of You'**, '**Because We Can'**, '**What About Now'** and '**What the Water Made Me'**.*
*In fact the whole album is Great until '**The Fighter'** song - doesn't really do it for me."*
Paul Nisbet (Inverness, Scotland, UK)

"Wow what an inspiration I just love to hear Jon Bon Jovi sing and of course it doesn't hurt to look at the best looking man on Earth all the time.
What a talented man! God gave him a very special gift, great genes, good looking, can play instruments and a vocalist very critique in his performance - it just comes natural.
*I've been listening to you ever since you started and I am thankful to say as long as you're on the radio or in concert and I'm here '**I'll Be There For You'**.*
I love you, God bless and thank you so much for sharing, please continue to do what God gave you the talent to do.
Always in my thoughts and prayers."
Tammy Fields (USA)

"Love this Album."
Claudia Flückiger (Biberist, Switzerland)

"My least favourite Bon Jovi album and hardly ever listen to it although you've inspired me to give it another go.
*It doesn't feel like a Bon Jovi album to me apart from a couple of exceptions. '**That's What the Water Made Me'** is awesome."*
Colin Gerrard (Stokenchurch, UK)

"Because We Can'."
Andrea Gibbons (Oshawa, Ontario, Canada)

"Absolutely love the song 'What's Left of Me' from this album."
Alan Harkin (East Kilbride, Scotland, UK)

We had 'Thick as Thieves' as our first dance at my wedding."
Chris Gibbins (Scunthorpe, UK)

"I LOVE THIS ALBUM!!!"
Ana Lopez (Arrecife, Lanzarote, Canary Islands, Spain)

*"**Welcome to Wherever You Are**' those words help me get thru my day sometimes. I love this band more then anything!!! My kids will always remember me singing Bon Jovi songs at the top of my lungs."*
Kelley Ladwig (Gilbert, Louisiana, USA)

"This album includes very deep and motivating thoughts.
I'm sad that it was the last one recorded with Mr Richie Sambora."
Olga Adamczyk (In the World)

"Love this album, the boys always get it right."
Debbie Woodward (Australia)

"Love the album. The lyrics are awesome.
Just that this is the album that reminds me when Richie never came back and unfortunately this is how I relate to it. But other than that, songs are great."
Irene Kirwan (Paterson, New Jersey, USA)

"Great album!! New And old songs fantastic!
*Played everyday on my way to work in yes car. Concert was amazing in Sunderland and we were treated to a rare '**Always**' performance.*
I'm 36 and missed their early year songs but I've listened to everyone since and own them all now.
They are my go to band to make me smile and get through bad times."
Laura Grieve (Middlesbrough, UK)

Spain

(Including My Favourite Concert)

"The '95 Wembley concert was extraordinary."
Lourdes García de Juan (Madrid, Spain)

Wembley Stadium, London, UK, 'These Days' Tour, 25th June 1995

Livin' on a Prayer
You Give Love a Bad Name
Wild in the Streets
Keep the Faith
Blood on Blood
Always

I'd Die for You
Blaze of Glory
Runaway
Dry County
Lay Your Hands on Me
I'll Sleep When I'm Dead
Bad Medicine
Bed of Roses
Hey God
These Days
Rockin' All Over the World
I Don't Like Mondays
Wanted Dead or Alive
Stranger in This Town
Someday I'll Be Saturday Night
This Ain't a Love Song

"Gijón 5 June '96."
Raul Suarez Gonzalez (Asturias, Spain)

"Bon Jovi, it makes me feel alive when I hear it, it gives me strength to overcome and without knowing him personally (hopefully), I feel like a friend always accompanies me."
Irene Prado Viñayo (Oviedo, Spain)

Burning Bridges

1) A Teardrop to the Sea............................5:08
2) We Don't Run.....................................3:19
3) Saturday Night Gave Me Sunday Morning.......3:23
4) We All Fall Down................................4:04
5) Blind Love.......................................4:47
6) Who Would You Die For.........................3:54
7) Fingerprints.....................................5:59
8) Life Is Beautiful................................3:22
9) I'm Your Man....................................3:44
10) Burning Bridges.................................2:44

Release Date: 21st August 2015
Producer: John Shanks, John Bon Jovi
Singles: 'We Don't Run',
'Saturday Night Gave Me Sunday Morning'

*"One of my faves from this is '**Who Would You Die For**'. The way Jon sings it & the music is really different. I really love the song but I can't decide if it is a super romantic song or super creepy."*
Joanna Does (Perth, Australia)

*"**We Don't Run**'... one of the best live songs ever!"*
Emma Ashcroft (Jacksonville, Florida, USA)

*"Love this album, one of my favourites, '**WE DON'T RUN**' is my ring tone on my phone, it's brilliant, and so rock, it should be out there.*
I fought cancer 3 times, been to BON Jovi live concerts their songs kept me strong, lost my husband, but their music keeps me going, had all clear from cancer after 17 years of fight still get checked but don't give up.
'IT'S MY LIFE, ALWAYS', xx."
Susan Jones (Pwllheli, Wales, UK)

"I love this CD."
Krystyna Zapędowska (Warsaw, Poland)

"I think for an album that was not very commercialised it is pretty awesome."
Katrina Righton (Perth, Australia)

"Waited so long for new album and loved it. Love all their albums."
Donna Watson (UK)

United Kingdom

(Including My Favourite Concert)

"I have loved Bon Jovi for 35 years... they are just simply the best band ever.

I have seen them play live 14 times now, I would love to go to more shows, but I just can't afford to but as long as I get to at least one of them when they tour U.K. then I'm happy.

I have had some great times watching Bon Jovi play live, I've been gold circle a few times, and got really close to the stage once in 2013. I've had Jon fly right above me on the New Jersey tour, at the Birmingham NEC arena.

Every single song is amazing and fits in with my life and there's always a song to suit your mood they are brilliant."
Alison Phelan (UK)

"I wish they would bring out all their love songs on one album, I would be in Bon Jovi heaven."
Suzanne Gardiner (Sudbury, Suffolk, UK)

"Loved Bon Jovi from day one, always have always will. Can't wait for 19th June to see him again at Anfield Stadium, Liverpool."
Sue Toyne (UK)

*"I've been a HUGE fan of Bon Jovi since they first came onto the scene.
I fell in love with Jon when I saw him on the video (shown on 'Top of the Pops') of '**Blaze of Glory**'.*

Seen them live several times - NEC Arena - Birmingham, Don Valley Stadium - Sheffield, Main Road Stadium - Manchester, Britannia Stadium - Stoke-on-Trent, Molyneaux Stadium - Wolverhampton, Etihad Stadium - Manchester, Old Trafford Cricket Ground - Manchester, Cardiff Stadium - Wales. Now awaiting tickets for Anfield Stadium - Liverpool on 19th June 2019. Can't wait.

Been about 6-feet away from Jon on his walk around the catwalk but couldn't quite reach to touch his hand (at Cardiff). Hoping to get nearer this time.

Greatest rock band (& singer) ever!!!"
Lynette Boydon (Ipstones, UK)

*I fell head over heels in love with Jon when a saw the '**Always**' vid, little did I know I'd been in love with him since '**Blaze of Glory**' but silly me didn't connect the dots!*

Back then I had 2 small kids and time for myself was unheard of, so it took me till '95 before I went to my 1st gig - it was magic but pity my hubby at the time didn't agree.

Then I got pen-pals and sent friendship letters that I had to keep secret cos my hubby (then) was totally jealous of my infatuation with Jon. To cut a long story short he ended up leaving me cos of my obsession, that's what he blamed anyway, I was much happier, just me my kids and Bon Jovi after all they were the love of my life.

When I got divorced and the papers came my ex had actually sited Jon Bon Jovi as the reason, pity Jon didn't come over for the decree on the divorce cos I'd have put him up for the night ha!!!!

Since then I've been to 12 gigs including Jon's solo gig. I have a partner now that may not love Bon Jovi as I do but he understands, so that's my story and all I can say now is Wembley gold circle here I come."
Joyce Maddick (Newcastle Upon Tyne, UK)

"Wembley '95, the best for me, even if I did melt in the heat."
Tania Johnson (Gloucester, UK)

"Wembley '95, my dad brought me and my best friend a ticket each as we were at university and couldn't afford it ourselves.
Got in early enough to make the front and Jon blew a kiss at me during the performance #swoon."
Sarah Miles (Linford, Essex, UK)

Wembley Stadium, London
25th June 1995
'These Days' Tour

Living on a Prayer
You Give Love a Bad Name
Wild in the Streets
Keep the Faith
Blood on Blood
Always
I'd Die for You
Blaze of Glory
Runaway
Dry County
Lay Your Hands on Me
I'll Sleep When I'm Dead
Bad Medicine
Bed of Roses
Hey God
These Days
Rockin' All Over the World
I Don't Like Mondays
Wanted Dead or Alive
Stranger in This Town
Someday I'll Be Saturday Night
This Ain't a Love Song

"*Sheffield City Hall, November 1986 - a proper rock crowd at a Jovi gig, not like today sadly.*"
Mark Lindley (Sheffield, UK)

"*Murrayfield Stadium 2011.*
*The '**Greatest Hits**' tour just after '**The Circle**' came out. Great show, great set.*"
Paul Nisbet (Inverness, Scotland)

"*The first one I ever went to Cardiff Millennium Stadium, 2001.*
Had so many emotions as I could not buy tickets before and my husband arranged it with the help of two friends.
It was awesome. I cried screamed sang and cheered new all the words to the songs had no voice for a week afterwards as I damaged my vocal cords, but it was amazing.
I'm going to my fourth concert in June to see them again I'm getting very excited. Who says you have to grow up at 50? Keep on rockin'."
Nikki Pope (Kempsey, Worcestershire, UK)

"*Milton Keynes 1993, '**I'll Sleep When I'm Dead**' Tour, first time I saw them. Also the O2 residency 2010 on '**The Circle**' Tour, first time for my daughter.*"
Sandra Wigley (Cranwell, UK)

"*As a relatively young fan I was the odd one in school for liking Bon Jovi. But they were more to me than just a band I liked. They were and still are my inspiration.*
Hearing how Jon came from singing in bars to asking a radio DJ to play his song and his dreams becoming a reality is the determination everyone should have in any walk of life.
*My parents had been playing Bon Jovi and other '80s bands music while I grew up but I only really fell in love when '**It's My Life**' was released when I was ten! It blew my mind.*
Now me and my Dad share our love for this band.
I have only been able to go to one of their concerts in my life but I will be going to more. I even got a rose tattoo with lyrics, which remind me to keep going whatever happens. Their music has got me through good and bad times and it will continue to do so.
*As Jon says '**Live for the fight...**'.*"
Rebecca Kenyon (Cleveleys, UK)

"Hamden Park – 'One Wild Night' tour when they came out of the elevator - class!!"
James Nolan (Aidrie, Scotland)

"Wembley '95 awesome."
Paula Foster (Reading, UK)

"My sister had the album, my cousins were in to Bon jovi all girls so I was slowly being brain washed age 10, was a fan till 2000.
Went in '96 to see them live with my sister, Maine Road, Manchester.
Seen Sambora twice as a support. Jovi not the same anymore.
Loved 'New Jersey' album as was too young for 'Slippery...' saw them '96. Then I lost interest. Still listen to first 6 albums."
Popeye Grib (Liverpool, UK)

"Love Bon Jovi, last night is the 3rd time I have seen them, they still rock it good. Both my daughters were brought up with Bon Jovi music and my granddaughter Willow who is one, was born to 'It's My Life'."
Lisa Haigh (Batley, UK)

"See you tomorrow Wembley!!!"
Vincent Bou (UK)

"For me it has to be at the old Wembley in 1995. First time I saw them live and I was just amazed by the energy and Jon's ability to get the whole enormous crowd going.
24 years and 9 concerts later? Still just as amazing and they still got it goin' on!"
Fiona Johnstone (Crawley, London, UK)

First saw them on MTV in 1986 - fell in love with Jon the minute I set eyes on him and he's been my hero since then.
Saw them for the first time in 1989, Birmingham NEC. WOW!
Brought my daughter up with their music and now she is a huge fan.
Jon and the band have got me out of some very dark places in my life and my daughters, the words of the songs and how Jon sings the songs.
My daughter and I are so dedicated we both have Bon Jovi tattoos.
Finally in 2013 managed to get daughter and myself to a concert, we shared the music together it was an amazing and emotional moment.
My grandson is only 18 months old and already a massive fan.
I'd just like to give the band a huge thank you for helping me and my family just hope they realise what effect they have on the fans."
Clare Louise, Carly and Harrison (UK)

"Yes I was there, and I'm showing my age now!
It was awesome, I had seen the band the previous summer at Milton
Keynes then again in the first week of Jan when they played 3 nights at
Wembley arena, I went to two of those shows and was surprised when
they suddenly announced a charity gig at the Hammersmith Odeon as it
was called back then.

I got my mum to get four tickets and was surprised she got them as they
took a few days to completely sell out! Anyway I mainly got them to see
what kind of show they would put on in an average size theater, I think at
the time the Hammersmith held about 3,000, we were about ten rows
back in the side stalls.

I sat in the pub next door with my mate and we joked about them having
special guest that would blow them off stage as the Milton Keynes gig
had the famous Steven Tyler and Joe Perry appearance which was
amazing. Little did we know what to expect would happen later that
evening?

On the way in I noticed a huge BBC Radio One van parked in the
alleyway next to the venue so I was expecting a live broadcast at some
point in the future, the bar was buzzing and packed with lots of Jovi
t-shirts and girls trying to wear very little despite the fact it was below
freezing outside!

An announcement said they would be on stage at I think 7.30 which was a
good sign, early start. We found our seats and I noticed the pub stage
they had was borrowed from The Quireboys who played there recently
and had supported Aerosmith the previous month with the same set.

The crowd went mad and kind of wondered what was happening as a solo
*Jon appeared to sing '**Goin' Back**', the section on the '**Access All Areas**'*
video sums it up nicely, he was nervous and we knew we were in for
something special.

What surprised me was that they then brought Richie out and sang
*'**Never Say Goodbye**' and '**Shooting Star**' then their two biggest hits, I*
couldn't work out what they were going to do for an encore now they had
*done '**Wanted…**' and '**Prayer…**'!*

*Next a very raw '**Love For Sale**' which was awesome followed by the*
curtains being pulled back to reveal the rest of the band. The first few
songs had cameramen with massive video cameras on their shoulders,
*which must have been for the '**Access…**' video.*

I don't remember them being there for the whole show which is a shame
because I would love to see a video of the show in a deluxe edition at
some point. The crowd were loving it, me being so young at the time
wanted to hear more Jovi songs so the covers was throwing me a bit (now
I love them).

The crowd went nuts when Jon said they were going to try out a new song **'Cadillac Man'** *I liked it and I felt like a special moment hearing a new song. I was convinced I would own a studio version of it by the summer! Three more Jovi songs followed* **'I'd Die For You'**, **'Wild in the Streets'** *and* **'Blood on Blood'** *then a beer break.*

Everyone was buzzing in the bar and it's true there were people that you wouldn't usually see at a Jovi gig, upstairs seemed to have a few older charity members of the Nordoff Robbins Trust who the evening was raising money for.

The curtain was pulled back and the band launched straight into **'The Boys are Back in Town'**; *if you listen to the bootleg you can hear Jon's "Alright" at the beginning, I love that as I can remember the excitement he had as he was jumping all over the front of the stage.*

'Bad Medicine' *and an awesome* **'You Keep Me Hangin' On'** *followed I remember that one got some big cheers at the end.* **'Silent Night'** *was next and then my favourite Jovi cover* **'Travelling Band'** *was next; I wish they still played that old Fogerty song.*

Next up was **'Fever/I Got The Fever'** *and then Jon introduced a London horn section that had joined them at Wembley Arena the week before, they started playing a brilliant version of* **'Social Disease'**.

The horn section left and I think Jon left the stage for a minute or so, there was a good tension in the air that something special was going to happen and it did!

That's when the "this man and this band" quote happened and out comes Jimmy Page, my mate from the pub almost fainted, he was and still is a massive Led Zep fan. You could almost feel the music critics in the audience writing about it and trying to slag it off but you couldn't it was such a fun moment seeing Jimmy with the band jamming and loving it. After that Jimmy left the stage to massive roars of the crowd why Jon started to wrap it up with **'Good Golly Miss Molly'** *then as a double whammy they brought Jimmy out again for the last track* **'With A Little Help From My Friends'**, *crowd go nuts again!*

Then they took their bows and left.

Everyone went home with big smiles on their face and knew they had seen something special, I have seen the band many times since including Astoria in '92 and Shepherds Bush in '02 but none was as good as that night in Hammersmith Odeon."

Mark Witherspoon (Hildenborough, UK)

"I love what you do Jon.
Amazing singer songwriter. Very talented man, keep doing what you do best.Love you always xx."

Becky Turner (UK)

"I've been a fan of Bon Jovi since I was 10 years old, 25 years.
Their music helped me through a lot of shit growing up.
I've been to see them 5 times, most recent in Wembley.
He is my absolute hero and I'm hoping he does another tour before he
retires. He's an amazing man, the restaurant he has, the wine he has and
the music he compiles. I don't know how he does it."
Deborah Elam (Great Clacton, Essex, UK)

"Bon Jovi are the soundtrack to my life.
Whatever has happened, whatever mood I'm in, there is an album to fit
my mind-set. After a bad day, a blast of Jovi in the car on the way home
and I can feel my stress melting away.
*I have been a fan since the '80s when I discovered '***Slippery...***', and have*
been lucky enough to see them live four times now.
Two of my three children are fans, and all three can quote lyrics back to
you.
For me, Bon Jovi are the whole package.
They are incredibly talented musicians, their music is thought provoking
at times and almost always uplifting. It makes you smile and it makes you
sing.
Jon's heart shines through his music and he comes over as a caring,
altruistic, sensitive man who can still rock a whole stadium 30 plus years
later.
Thank you Bon Jovi."
Zoe Sutton (Peterborough, UK)

*"I have been a fan since '***Runaway***'.*
Bon Jovi always reflect on current situations in the world and their own
personal relationships, yet there is always something we can relate to as
fans.
I went to my 1st concert in Coventry this year... a dream come true!"
Kathy Pilkington (UK)

"First time ever saw the guys live 1986 - small concert hall in the UK,
then over the years they got bigger 'n' bigger and last month had an
amazing hospitality view of them at Anfield.
I could not believe I was actually seeing them live again - lost count how
many times - roll on the next time.
Aiming on saving and seeing them in the USA with my pen pal in Florida
who I met through 'Backstage With Bon Jovi' over 35 yrs ago - never met
her yet, but where better than at a concert with the guys who brought us
together across the Atlantic."
Jane Geldart (UK)

Anfield Stadium, Liverpool, 19th June 2019 'This House Is Not For Sale' Tour

This House Is Not For Sale
Raise Your Hands
You Give Love a Bad Name
Born to Be My Baby
Whole Lot of Leavin'
Lost Highway
Runaway
We Weren't Born to Follow
Have a Nice Day
Keep the Faith
Amen
I'll Be There for You
Blood on Blood
We Don't Run
Wanted Dead or Alive
Lay Your Hands on Me
Captain Crash & the Beauty Queen From Mars
I'll Sleep When I'm Dead
Bad Medicine
These Days
Livin' on a Prayer
Birthday
Twist & Shout

"I've been a fan of Jon Bon Jovi since day one.
I've brought 3 beautiful daughters up listening to all his songs. When my youngest daughter was aged just 3 she stood on a stage and sang every word to 'I'll Be There For You'... I can't tell you how proud I was of her and even today all my girls aren't shy at belting out Bon Jovi songs."
Jayne Walkland (Sheffield, UK)

"Wembley '95 absolutely hands down the best I've seen.
'These Days' tour xx."
Debbie Bonjovi (Merthyr Tydfil, Wales, UK)

"San Siro 2013 - what a venue and seeing Jon's emotion at the fan choreography display in the crowd was priceless!
Hyde Park 2013 is up there too, my first concert where I made it to front row and got a wink from Jon during the show!"
Naomi Booker (UK)

"Best concert ever - Wembley 1995 when they knocked MJ off the number one spot!!! Totally phenomenal show!"
Emma Louise Adams (UK)

"Any in the '80s and '90s."
Deborah Hick (UK)

"June 13 2001, Huddersfield, England, the 'One Wild Night' tour.
It was a silver wedding anniversary gift from my husband. Best gift I ever had! A fantastic night. My first ever Rock concert too!"
Christine Beardshall (Doncaster)

"Madison Sq, Gardens, Feb 2011.
I'm from Scotland, and my husband surprised me with a trip to NYC for my 40th Birthday. That was great enough, but then surprised me again when we got there when we went to pick up tickets to see Bon Jovi that night!!
I burst into tears and the poor girl giving out the tickets didn't know what to do!
We went both nights because my husband panicked when the e-mail to pick up the tickets for the first night didn't arrive, so he bought tickets for the next night too. Said to me in NYC –
"so we can either go again or sell them..." - eh, we'll be going again!!!
So, been to see Bon Jovi many, many times, loved them all, but that one ticked something off my bucket list so that stands out."
Kirsteen Macdonald (Scotland)

Madison Square Garden New York, USA, 24th February 2011, 'Live 2011' Tour

Last Man Standing
You Give Love a Bad Name
Born to Be My Baby
We Weren't Born to Follow
Lost Highway
When We Were Beautiful
It's My Life
Runaway
Superman Tonight
The More Things Change
We Got It Goin' On
Bad Medicine
(You Want to) Make a Memory
I'll Be There for You
Something for the Pain
Someday I'll Be Saturday Night
Who Says You Can't Come Home
I'll Sleep When I'm Dead
No Apologies
Have a Nice Day
Keep the Faith
In These Arms
Wanted Dead or Alive
Livin' on a Prayer

"My first concert was Hyde park in 2011.
I had waited since I was 14 to see them. I was almost 40 when I finally made it due to my health.
I was in so much shock when he walked on stage, I just stood there.
My best memory ever.
He was on stage for 3 hours. The set list was awesome. Once a Jovi girl, always a Jovi girl. Will live with me forever."
Donna Brimson (Portsmouth)

"Donington '87, when they really hit the big time. From 2 thousand capacity Odeon shows to headlining to over 80 thousand fans.
*His voice was shot, Richie slipped on the steps at the start of '**Raise Your Hands**' and loads of Metalheads were telling Jon to jump when he was stood on the stage roof when they played '**Let it Rock**' (with a bit of 'We Will Rock You' thrown in). Didn't bother us Jovi fans though, I was hoarse for a week after.*
Saw them 7 times in '88 and '89 on the 2 UK legs and the MK Bowl."
David Jones (Warsop, UK)

"San Siro Milan 2013.
Jon was speechless when the Italian fans displayed all their '30 years' banners. We got something like 5 encores. Fantastic show."
Michael Dewsnap (UK)

"Opening the O2. Jon was so up for it after missing out on opening the new Wembley.
Wembley 2019 – a special place for Jon, Phil was on fire and the crowd were up for it from the first note! Memorable night!"
Julie Pinkney Hoyle (UK)

"Milton Keynes Bowl, 2006.
Bon Jovi were meant to play Wembley when it re-opened but construction wasn't finished so the concert was moved.
That didn't stop the guys though, they were full of energy with an absolutely amazing set list followed by 2 encores.
That will always hold a special place in my heart because although it was my third Bon jovi concert it was my brothers first, I'd gotten him tickets for his birthday the previous year and having him by my side rocking out to our favourite band was just amazing."
Dario Briatore (Loughborough, UK)

"June 29th 2011 RDS Arena Dublin.
The day before the concert I met Jon near our hotel and had a photo with him, never dreamt that would happen! Then ended up spending the afternoon at a bar with the stage manager and crew, what a day and to top it off a great show!! Will never forget it."
Gemma Vincent (Milton Abbas)

"Birmingham NEC 1988.
Jon held my hand all through 'Wanted...' - still in love now."
Tracy O'Neill (Stourport)

"Went to Wembley 2019 on crutches, what a night we had, there was no way I was going to miss the guys."
Suzanne Gardiner (Sudbury, Suffolk)

"I went to see JBJ at Liverpool in July.

I've been a fan since I was 15, now I'm 40 - seen him every time he's been to the UK.

He was fantastic he came on to the stage and I cried, yes at 40 I cried I was so happy and excited. Jon bon Jovi and the lads knew how to throw a gig.

He will never lose his touch it was amazing from start to finish. He had the crowd singing all the time it was the best.

2 and half hours he sang for. When he went off I cried again. He's a true singer and a true gent to his wife and kids - you don't get many famous singers still married to they school sweetheart. Love them as a family xxx"

Angela Holden (Manchester)

*"Lucky enough to have seen Bon Jovi 14 times. Followed them since 1986 after buying '**Slippery When Wet**'.*
Can't pick one gig, they've all been amazing.
Watched them at different stadiums across the UK including Scotland, 02 London, Manchester, Stoke-on-Trent and Milton Keynes."
Debbie Leese (UK)

"First time I have ever seen Bon Jovi was at Coventry in June 2019, and I'm 52, so a late comer.
Absolutely fantastic gig, brilliant atmosphere too. Everyone seemed to be having a great time, singing and dancing. Well worth the long travel home and only getting 2 hours sleep before getting back up for work.
I hope I can see them live again one day.
And I absolutely love Phil X!!!"
Elaine Priestley (Skipton)

"First saw, BON JOVI live 1993 Milton Keynes, first chance I had (children, mortgage etc.) been a fan for ever, so many fantastic live shows but that one will always be special.
Apart from that, the Cardiff, 2001, was so very much special, being WELSH, it was lovely to see them in my country."
Susan Jones (Pwllheli, Wales, UK)

"My first concert was Villa Stadium June 2013, I will not forget that! I'll always say it was the best one for me because it was my first, but I equally enjoyed the concert in Coventry this year."
Emma Hinde (Reading)

"Monsters of Rock, Donington Park 1988, first class."
Vinny Maguire (UK)

"Amazing band, come a very long way enjoyed every performance love the songs so deep and entertaining rock band god bless the band and their family.
Love to see Jon Bon Jovi again - went to Wembley 21st June 2019."
Rosemary Riches (Great Yarmouth)

"Every concert I've been to, is always first class, amazing atmosphere, and Jon, well he's certainly got the audience hooked from start to finish, #bonjoviforever&always."
Tracey Gregson (UK)

"Been a fan since '86.
Have been to so many gigs. Heard Richie play 'Stranger in This Town' and the hair at the back of my neck stood up.
But my best memory is when I got a VIP ticket brilliant day and when I met Jon in London when he was promoting 'Destination Anywhere' at Virgin Radio and managed to give him a skey n du would love to find out if he still has it."
Rose Milne (Aberdeen)

"Best thing since sliced bread, still got the wow factor."
Amanda Enderby (Attleborough, Norfolk)

"Back in the day when you had to be in the fan club to get wrist bands for the front enclosure, of course things didn't go smoothly even then.
In August 2000 I borrowed a fan card so my boyfriend could get in front with me, all I new what to do at the time was to show my fan card at the entrance to the front and we'd get in, but no! Nobody told me that we had to go to a booth to get wrist-bands.
I found out that the same had happened to a lot the day before, a stink was made bout it and they did get in but on that day I didn't, I was very frustrated, anyway am rambling on here, later in the week me and my daughter went to Gateshead stadium and that day I made sure I got my wrist band. My daughter however had to be at the front of the queue and

run like hell cos they let the 1st few hundred in the front and put wrist-bands on them so she was with me.

Back in them days was the best, the front enclosure was Great, you could actually move around and I must say EVERY Bon Jovi concert has been FANTASTIC.

This year however me and my daughter made our way to Wembley. First time I was there was '95, We paid for the gold circle first time, in the past I've been in the seats and standing but wanted to do gold circle this time thinking it would be like back in the late '90s, but I found to my dismay that practically half the pitch was gold circle cos like I keep saying the front back in the day was a lot smaller.

Anyway, with me being short I didn't see much of my hero Jon except on the screens, Fantastic concert, the best one yet till the next one. W

*When Jon sang '**Always**' for the encore, I could of cried but my daughter was determined I'd see my beloved Jon so she got a very kind stranger to get me up on his shoulders and Wow it was amazing.*

*I've since watched '**Always**' from Wembley on YouTube and I can see myself so I look at myself as being famous cos I am on a Bon Jovi video the BEST BAND IN THE WORLD now that's me done HA!*

By the way I'm 62!"

Joyce Maddick (Newcastle Upon Tyne)

"Huddersfield Stadium, England – it's called John Smiths Stadium now, it wasn't back then but can't remember what it was called - long time ago!"

Yvonne Nugent (Ilfracombe, UK)

*"I've been a fan ever since '94, when my neighbours daughter was blasting '**Always**', I was 9 years old it was then that I discovered Bon Jovi.*

I had to wait 16 years, but I finally got my chance to see them in concert. 2000 in London was just amazing, seeing the band that I grew to love perform all my favourites songs live was a 'dream come true'.

Since then I made it my mission in life to attend a concert every time they went on tour.

Over the years I "treated" myself to such things as golden circle tickets diamond circle tickets and even the backstage tour, where my greatest memory was holding (and playing) Richie's guitar before he came on stage."

Dario Briatore (Loughborough)

Where to start?

*I discovered my ultimate Band in the early '80s, when I was around 19/20. I remember insisting on having the '**Slippery When Wet**' Album for my 21st Birthday, this was on Vinyl. I later got it on C.D. Obviously I have every C.D going!*

I truly resonate with his music, the lyrics mean more than words to me! The whole of Stafford know I'm Jovi mad, can't get enough of them!!!

My Mother actually liked my music as I always played it, whether in the house or in the car, so she got into Bon Jovi (which isn't difficult).

Both of my children have been brought up listening to Bon Jovi, & now even my Grandchildren are in to them, so that's 4 generations loving his music.

I'm now registered disabled, but love to play darts. My official darting name is 'Jovi Girl'. If I could get any Sponsorship from the great Man himself, this would make my life complete! I'd certainly like to help him help me by advertising The Soul kitchen or The Bon Jovi Foundation on my Darts shirts!

I've seen no end of his Concerts & I'm completely addicted to this amazing band!"

Mandie Howard (Stafford)

"Me and my friend saw Bon Jovi years ago, it was back in the day when u got to the concert by bus.

It was amazing! We all sang their songs on way home.

Since then, me and my sister have seen them all over UK -O2 Arena, Coventry, Edinburgh, Wembley, Stoke and Milton Keynes.

We are true fans and still get great Bon Jovi goodies on my birthday and Christmas from hubby and sister."

Lisa Smith (UK)

"The gig in Tallinn last June was amazing!

It was the first time Bon Jovi had ever played Estonia. The atmosphere was brilliant.

The gig was played at the Song Festival Grounds, which holds a special place in Estonian hearts due to independence in 1991. I flew from the UK to see them, to link my Estonian heritage and my love and passion for Bon Jovi."

Tammy Meras (UK)

Tallinna Lauluväljak, Tallinn, Estonia, 2nd June 2019 'This House Is Not for Sale' Tour

This House Is Not for Sale
Raise Your Hands
You Give Love a Bad Name
Born to Be My Baby
Whole Lot of Leavin'
Lost Highway
Runaway
We Weren't Born to Follow
Have a Nice Day
Keep the Faith
Amen
Bed of Roses
It's My Life
We Don't Run
These Days
Lay Your Hands on Me
God Bless This Mess
Blood on Blood
We Got It Goin On
Bad Medicine
Wanted Dead or Alive
Livin' on a Prayer

"Wembley 2019 amazing! W
Waited long time for him to come back to England, they didn't
disappoint. Shame about Ritchie, but amazing just the same.
Magic night spent with a special person Tom Howlett xxx."
Lyndsey Palmer (UK)

"Wow been a fan for over 30 years love the band today just as much as I did then.
Seen them live 4 times loved everyone.
Miss Ritchie being in band, him and Jon playing guitar together is something else!
Thanks for the music guys keep rocking it."
Karen Brookes (Broadheath, Cheshire)

"My all time favourite Bon Jovi song is 'Always', I sing it at the top of my lungs.
I first heard it in my teenage years, and I have always wanted it to be my first dance song at my Wedding.
This song gives me goosebumps every time."
Jenni Bishop (Plymouth)

This House Is Not For Sale

1) This House Is Not for Sale.........3:36
2) Living With the Ghost.............4:44
3) Knockout..........................3:29
4) Labor of Love.....................5:03
5) Born Again Tomorrow.............3:33
6) Roller Coaster.....................3:40
7) New Year's Day....................4:27
8) The Devil's in the Temple..........3:19
9) Scars on This Guitar...............5:06
10) God Bless This Mess................3:23
11) Reunion...........................4:14
12) Come On Up to Our House.........4:35

Release Date: 4th November 2016
Producer: Jon Bon Jovi, John Shanks
Singles: 'This House Is Not for Sale', 'Knockout', 'Labor of Love', 'Born Again Tomorrow', 'When We Were Us', 'Walls' (2018 Reissue)

"God I love this album. So many lyrics that mean so much to me!!"
Sarah Miles (Linford, Essex, UK)

"Awesome album, play it all the time."
Lorraine Birds (UK)

"Revision of Bon Jovi's career. So rocking.
Incredible that they are still so awesome to make songs like that."
Olga Adamczyk (Poland)

*"**This House Is Not for Sale**'...*
One of my absolute favourite albums to listen to.
*The message from the title track talking of strong roots, the song '**Knockout**' gives the sense of empowerment, where as people in a relationship can most certainly relate to '**Rollercoaster**'.*
*My absolute favourite has to be '**Scars on This Guitar**'... a relationship between a man and his instrument, without each other neither could make music, so poetic."*
Dario Briatore (Loughborough, UK)

"Grown up with Bon Jovi music since I was 13 as I approach 50 their music has grown with me as it has with thousands of others.
*'**THINFS**' has been the next step on my stepping stones of life."*
Tracy O'Neill (Stourport, UK)

"The thing that stands out on this album is David's vocals. He makes you not miss Richie at all. This is David's album."
Dana Cooper (Martinsburg, West Virginia, USA)

"Their music, their words... are my life.
Not a day goes by that I don't hear their music somewhere, some place."
Marcella Meadors (Salt Lake City, Utah, USA)

"Took me a while to get my head round this one.
*Reminded me of how I felt when I first heard '**It's My Life**'. It felt different. Couldn't listen to one song all the way through. Three years later it's one of my favourites.*
*'**Reunion**', '**Rollercoaster**', '**Walls**', '**God Bless This Mess**' and '**THINFS**' are my faves."*
Emma Ashcroft (Jacksonville, Florida, USA)

"Love it."
Yvonne Young (Cumbernauld, Scotland, UK)

*"The Tidal debut, raw, NYC, '**THINFS**'."*
Nikki Fazzaro (In the World)

"Absolutely love this album and I also got to see them in concert - best day of my life, Jovi girl for life!"
Fawn Columbus (Morgan, Minnesota, USA)

"Absolutely love this album their music has matured and I love it."
Katrina Righton (Australia)

"This album is by far, my favorite.
They are songs that you can relate to and they give a message at the same time. Love this album."
Caryn Hurd (Camdenton, Missouri, USA)

United States of America

(Including My Favourite Concert)

"I saw him in Utica, NY in 1987.
Long hair, did my fav song in pink curlers, bathrobe and pink slippers lol!
And Cinderella opened for him, just amazing oxox"
D. Farr (USA)

"It's amazing just how many Bon Jovi fans I've come across in the last 20 years, and how one man can bring so many smiles to so many faces around the world....
I walk into my bank and sit down for my notary public appt. & the handsome young man takes one look at the picture on my debit card & says.... "IS THAT JON BON JOVI??!" I started laughing and said "yep it sure is!!"
Needless to say, we spent the next hour exchanging stories about how we became fans, our favorite albums, what concerts we had been to... He said his parents were die-hard fans and he had grown up listening to Bon Jovi and knew all the songs by heart.
I said "I couldn't wait to tell my son, that was about his age, he wouldn't feel so alone thinking he was the only one that got dragged along to a Jovi concert and sang along to all the songs in the car with mom!!!"
He chuckled and said "nope, he's not alone!!! Bon Jovi rocks!!!" #MadeMyDay."
Melissa A. Jaynes (Salem, Utah, USA)

"Well I have been a Fan for 36 years since I was 14.
I was walking down the hall one day and my Sister was watching MTV and I stopped in my tracks and asked
"who is that?"
She said "a group called BON JOVI I think?" and I said "no who is that?" and I pointed to John and she said "that's John BON JOVI", they were singing 'She Don't Know Me' and I fell in love!
A few days later they were on American Bandstand and they never looked back.
They have always and I truly mean this always been a part of my life I listen to them everyday and let me just say when you're feeling down about something all you have to do is look at picture or a clip of John and his Sweet Smile will lift your spirits!
I love this Man as a Rock Star but he is so much more than that to me! The Community work and the giving back to others means so much more to me than he will ever know!
Thank you for all the music memories over the last 36 years you only get better and better and we love you more everyday if that's even possible! I love BON JOVI 1983-2019."
Paula Reid (Fountain Inn, South Carolina, USA)

"I'm a Jersey girl.
Was once in a revolving hotel door in Boston, just me 'n' Jon... AHHHHH ONE OF MY FAVORITE MEMORIES.
The band is the best. I worked at a Radio Station in Boston (WBCN). I THANK YOU ALL."
Katharine Dudek (Merrimac, Massachusetts, USA)

"It was on the 'New Jersey' tour...
At this concert in Chicago on 3/24/1989, was the first time I met Jon! Memories forever..."
Sonya Curtis (Round Lake Beach, Illinois, USA)

"I've never been to one, but I was able to watch parts of the Moscow Peace festival. That was insane."
Cyndi Lane (Bakersfield, California, USA)

"Slippery When Wet' in Orlando.
It was the first concert at the Orlando Arena back in the '80s.
It was awesome! Not a bad seat to be had & I got great pics."
Kelly Hillstrom (La Crosse, Wisconsin, USA)

"My name is Denise Treglio and I have been an avid follower of Bon Jovi since before they became Bon Jovi.

*When I was a senior in high school in 1983 I used to listen 103.5 WAPP. They were doing some thing on the station where they played songs by some newcomers and I had heard '**Runaway**' by Jon Bon Jovi. It wasn't just the song, but his voice…it just did something to me, so much so that I had to have more.*

So, I contacted WAPP and requested the song. Of course, my request wasn't met. So I became persistent.

I left the phone number of the radio station by the phone and would have my mom call at least once a day while I was school and request the song. When I got home from school or work (sometimes I went to work right from school) I would call myself and make the request. I called everyday for a few weeks if my memory serves me right... and the days I had the time. Sometimes I would be calling from the phone in my room in one ear and have the long stretchy cord from the kitchen phone glued to the other ear and would simultaneously call twice in a row requesting it. I won't lie - I called every hour in hopes that they would play the song.

I had no idea who the singer was other than his name, didn't know what he looked like, knew nothing other than hearing that song and that listening to that voice that truly made goosebumps go up and down my spine.

One day, I get home from work, did my usual –

"mom, did you call them for me?"

"Of course I did."

And as I was just relaxing a few minutes before hopping into the shower so I could go out for a bit, my phone rings and when I answered it, I almost had a heart attack. It was one of the DJs from WAPP.

He asked me if I was Denise Miller... I did all I could to not scream 'YES' in his ear.

He said, "listen, we know you have been calling, AND CALLING, and we are going to do you a favor. You have 5 minutes to hang up and call all your friends and family and tell them to tune into WAPP because in 5 minutes we are going to play the song for you. Oh, and Denise, do us a favor, STOP CALLING!"

So, I did just as he suggested... called as many friends as I could (had my brother call from houseline as well) and the station came through and the song was played.

They even said my name when the DJ said, "Denise, this one's for you".

I was a die-hard fan even more so.

I have been lucky enough to see them 5 times, one of those times I was 6 months pregnant with my first child in 1986. But one of the best times was seeing the now formed band, Bon Jovi at Great Adventure in Jackson, NJ on June 28, 1985.

I was there with 3 friends and I wore a black t-shirt that was a bit oversized and had the word RELAX on it in hot pink... anyway, we were really only there to see the band.

We got up pretty close to the stage, we were maybe 15 feet from them. Well, we started talking to these guys that were there and one of my friends had to dare me to do it...

Rule #1 don't dare me. She dared me to throw my bra up on stage. Now I am what people call a well endowed woman, and back then in 1985 I was just 20 years old... the band is playing, we are having a great time, Jon was as hot as that golden voice of his... so I did it.

I took it off, flung it up on stage, and it landed on Jon's feet! My friends still have the same memory, so as it goes, Jon picked it up, held it up we do believe he said 'HOLY SHIT' (into the mike mid song) and I was so embarrassed (which I don't really get) that we started to work our way out of the concert area, before they were even over.

As we got close to the exit Jon was on the mike saying –

"Hey 'Relax' come back here I know it was you!".

Despite my fun bags flapping in the hot non-existent breeze, it truly made my night.

Over the years, I have always stayed true to my love for Jon and the band. I had some trying times, as do many, and each album had a song or songs that were significant for me during those times.

I got married in 1986, had a daughter in 1987 and she died at 10 months old from pneumonia in 1988... and Bon Jovi was one of the few things that gave me any little bit of comfort.

I have gone on to marry 2 more times and my second husband was so jealous of Jon that he tried to forbid me to listen to my music, and trust me when I say he did everything to sabotage it, he even smashed my vinyl's of Bon Jovi, and tore apart the cassettes. He would tell our 2 small kids that I was not allowed to say the name Bon Jovi, or Jon Bon Jovi or listen to their music... yes he was pathetic.

Now husband #3 has no problem with Jon.

He even paid $400 for two tickets for me to see him back in 2003. I was supposed to see them when then came out to Kansas, (yes I am a Jersey Girl now living out in the Land of Oz) back in 2010, but I gave my money for my tickets to my husband so he could see his mom at the end of 2009 before she passed... so I never got to see them after 2005.

But I still buy the albums, watch the TV specials, have some of the books, have memorabilia and even have a license plate and license plate frame and sticker on my truck.

I wasn't able to replace my vinyl records or the cassettes, but I have 'em all on cd, and even duplicates of some. When I need a pick me up or just for no reason, I pop in a Bon Jovi cd and blast it when I can... this **'Runaway'** *loves the idea of a* **'Bed of Roses'** *with* **'One Last Cigarette'** *and visions of Jon in her head.*

I figured I would tell you why my second husband was so jealous of Jon. When #2 and I started dating, I am sure he heard 'Bon Jovi' or 'Jon Bon Jovi' come out of my mouth quite a bit. At that time, I had also lived 20 minutes from Jon's house in Sayerville, NJ, and I knew which house was his soooooo...

I guess I took the ride there at least 3 times a week and drove around the block a few times to go past the house at least 4 or 5 times each time.

Then MTV was doing the contest to give away Jon's house and yes, of course I entered. I entered it exactly 275 times... sadly, no, I didn't win it.

But the day of the giveaway (March 30, 1989) I talked my boss into letting me off work early. My intention was to go there and see it all go down. When I got to where I had to turn off Rt. 35 it was pretty much barricaded, but I had gone there so many times over those months prior that I told the cops that I lived there, proceeded to give them an address (which incidentally was across the street from Jon's). Dumb cops let me in, and I drove up as close as I could, and yes I parked in someone's driveway too.

My ex was livid when he found out I entered the contest, and he hated that I would go past his house. He was even more annoyed that I got out of work early to show up the day of the giveaway. He felt like he competed with Jon for me, which in retrospect, is pretty friggin' hilarious if you ask me.

When he and I had our second child, a son, he was due originally on Jon's birthday (March 2nd) and Jon and Dorothea had just had Jesse Feb. 19, 1995... I had even wanted to name my son Jesse as well, until my ex thought he was funny and said only way we would is if his middle name was James, and I was not having my son named after an outlaw. My son ended up a few days early - Feb.26 - and we named him Christopher.

Yes, looking back, there were times I did torment my ex with Jon's or the bands name, but it wasn't every single time or all the time. It still gave him no right to do what he did to me with my Bon Jovi albums or memorabilia. I have had to replace it all and some of it I was unable to, but it's all good.

Got rid of the ex, and my hubby #3 of almost 17 years even let me have a huge assed poster of Jon on our bedroom wall...so I win."

Denise Treglio (Wellington, Kansas, USA)

Great Adventure Amusement Park
Jackson, NJ
'7800° Fahrenheit' Tour
28th June 1985

Tokyo Road
Breakout
Only Lonely
She Don't Know Me
Bang Bang
Shot Through the Heart
Silent Night
Runaway
Get Ready

"Mine was the 'Circle Tour' made plans for the family made a promise and kept it, only thing was Dad didn't get to go, he had passed.
But me and my girls went and had an awesome time, we had VIP passes but were not able to meet with the band.
Bon Jovi put on a hell of a great show and we were there all day just to see them. Loves to all.
Rock on forever."
Kathy Bogard (Louisville, Kentucky, USA)

"Which ever one I was fortunate enough to be at."
Buffy Reid (Fountain Inn, South Carolina, USA)

*"**This House is Not for Sale**' tour April 21st 2018 in Charlotte NC. It was special because it was my daughter's first concert and to share that moment with her is something I'll never forget."*
Melissa Blevins Gordon (Yadkinville, North Carolina, USA)

Spectrum Center, Charlotte, NC, 'This House Is Not For Sale' Tour, 21st April 2018

This House Is Not For Sale
Raise Your Hands
You Give Love a Bad Name
Whole Lot of Leavin'
Lost Highway
Born to Be My Baby
Who Says You Can't Go Home
It's My Life
We Weren't Born to Follow
Runaway
We Got It Goin'On
Keep the Faith
Amen
Bed of Roses
Lay Your Hands on Me
Living With the Ghost
I'll Sleep When I'm Dead
Bad Medicine
(You Want to) Make a Memory
Wanted Dead or Alive
Livin' on a Prayer

"In 2003, I saw Bon Jovi in Philly.
It was floor seats, I could see the whole stage without turning, and when Jon took his jacket off I could see his superman tattoo.
I was 6 month pregnant and my daughter wouldn't stop moving for the whole concert. I have been a fan for 30 yrs."
Michelle Newton (Penn Yan, New York)

"Bon Jovi w/ Skid Row opened in Houston TX Back in the late '80s early '90s Houston Summit or Coliseum Great Show!!!"
Patricia A. Pilcher (USA)

*"Every single one I've attended. I'm at 6 if I count Jon's **'Runaway in Vegas'** last year."*
Sandra Horton (California, USA)

"Jon opening concert at Met Life stadium in home state of Jersey."
Sue Haydu (Pittstown, New Jersey, USA)

"I went to 5 they were all great."
Pam Klemish (Bay City, Michigan, USA)

"1988 Bon Jovi and Skid Row at Alpine Valley—first time seeing them when I was 11 years old and I will never forget that night!
*2003, Madison, WI on the **'Bounce'** tour with the Goo Goo Dolls. I was 25 years old, my husband had been killed in a motorcycle accident about 6 months prior.*
*The songs **'Everyday'** and **'Bounce'** were my daily reminder that things would be ok and life would go on. I had 7th row seats with my best friends and family. I was crazy and had a water bra with my name and phone number written on it. My brother in law chucked that thing on stage and hit Jon dead center—he caught it, held it up and got a goofy grin and then tossed it aside and went on singing.*
The next day my phone rang and it was a guy who called himself 'Big Worm', claiming he was a roadie for the band and telling me he would get me free tickets or backstage passes if I would meet up with him. Needless to say I passed on that lol but it was a memory I will never forget.
I have loved Bon Jovi since I first discovered them in 1988 and the love affair with the band is still just as strong today. I have seen them 6 times in concert and loved every minute of it!"
Crystal Sternard (Egg Harbor, Wisconsin, USA)

"All of them!!!"
Ana Diaz (Mexicali, Baja, California, USA)

"The only one I was able to go to, in Hartford back in 2008? I think."
Linda McKernan (Bloomfield, Connecticut, USA)

"It was on the 'New Jersey' tour...
At this concert in Chicago on 3/24/1989 was the first time I met Jon!
Memories forever..."
Sonya Curtis (Round Lake Beach, Illinois, USA)

"All of them!!! The 'Runaway' cruise in April and May 19th 2010."
Lea Leiby (USA)

"My favorite concert shirt was the 'We're back kicking ass..'
New Jersey' tour shirt...
Favorite show was March 2nd 1992 here in Detroit and if you know the
date you know why it was a great show."
Brian Hughes (Detroit, Michigan, USA)

"Because We Can' tour! @ Mohegan Sun, 3 straight hours of show!"
Debbie Ford (USA)

"July 12, 2008 Central Park New York City - Free Concert for Bon Jovi
Fan Club Members.
Only a few select bands have had the honor to have played on the Great
Lawn.
No other band in the world cares for their fans as Bon Jovi and that is
why they are the best loved band in the World with 30+ years and still
rocking them all!"
Bev Bunis (USA)

"October 4, 1986... opening for 38 Special at Roberts Stadium in
Evansville, Indiana!
I love every concert, but this is my favorite because I worked my way
down to the stage and Jon shook my hand! It was one of the most
exhilarating moments of my young life!
I was 18, a freshman in college, and got to touch the sexiest man I had
ever seen! WOW!"
Regina Ritter Harrison (Princeton, Kentucky, USA)

"That's a toss up between the 'Slippery When Wet' tour & the 'New Jersey' Tour & the 'Bounce' tour!
I'd have to tell you why in private!!"
Locaa Valle (USA)

"Because We Can."
Pamela Anderson Jones (Kirkwood, Illinois, USA)

"July 2006 in Giants Stadium, in the pouring rain.
Jon looked up at the heavens and proclaimed
"Don't even think about f – – – ing with me when I'm in Jersey."
Alfonso Castillo (Valley Stream, New York, USA)

"Have a Nice a Day' tour 2006 - Greenville SC.
It was one of the first shows after Heather and Richie split.
Felt bad for the situation but Jon seemed a bit like he had something to
SAY and they performed the daylights out of those songs."
Melissa Martin Collins (USA)

"My favorite band in the world!
Book should be titled 'From Living On a Prayer, to Wanted Dead or Alive!' Cause, all their shows always sell out!
I've seen them when they were touring for their 1st album Bon Jovi, and they opened up for 38 special, and then again when they opened up for Ratt.
Was there for 'Slippery When Wet', all the way to 'This House Is Not For Sale'. But, my personal favorite was the 'New Jersey' tour! Had front row seats... I could tell you some stories...wild times."
Leslie D.Valle (USA)

"Been a big fan every since they came out always of one day to go to one of there shows I guess you could say by all the crying I did over the year I seen them once but I wasn't close enough to be pulled up on stage.
I guess there's a reason for that, I think I would of died but I got to see them and I'll always remember we sang every song, where I couldn't talk for days always and forever.
Love Jon Bon Jovi, puts a smile on my face. All my friends with out me telling them if you asked who's Lucy's love they all would say Jon Bon Jovi."
Lucy N Donnie Terry (USA)

"Love him, he is so good and still going strong."
Janet Valerie Cross (Winchester, Kentucky, USA)

"WENT TO THE COWPALACE IN SAN FRANCISCO WOW!!!! IT WAS ONE HELL OF A CONCERT!!!! WILL NEVER FORGET!!!"
Diana Araiza Atkins (Fremont, California, USA)

*"I've been a fan since 1985 and the '**Bon Jovi**' album.*
I have seen them in concert 6 times and have been all the way down front shaking Jon's hand to the farthest away seat!
It didn't matter; every show was great!
To me, there has always been a real connection to their music, after all, I am a real- life Gina and I married my Tommy!"
Regina Ritter Harrison (Princeton, Kentucky, USA)

"Love Bon Jovi. Great band have been a fan for many years.
I like that Jon has a huge heart and built homes for the homeless and his wife created the 'Soul Kitchen' to help people in need and you work for your dinner or pay or pay it forward. That says a lot about giving.
Hope to get to see Bon Jovi one day live in US. Have a nice day!"
Patty Killingbeck (Danville, Illinois, USA)

"I listened to a certain kind of music in high school (rock 'n' roll) of course and Bon Jovi was at the top of that list.
Their music got me through heartbreaks, and was just all around what I played to lift me up through anything.
*I graduated in 1993, also gave birth to my oldest daughter, so I found out who my real friends were really fast. That same child just won her battle with cancer and I was able to take her and my youngest daughter of 16 to see Bon Jovi in concert back in 2017 '**This House is Not For Sale**' Tour to celebrate that as I have passed on my love for Bon Jovi music and it was their first concert ever and The Best Concert!*
So Thank You Bon Jovi for giving us those memories that will last us a lifetime."
Amy Holliman (Rockfield, Kentucky, USA)

"I have followed Bon Jovi since 1983.
Jon is an awesome man whom I would like 2 meet 1 day.
I luv Bon Jovi - keep rockin'."
Brenda Headley (Coshocton, Ohio, USA)

*"2008 the '**Lost Highway**' Tour."*
Roger Braun (Glendale, Arizona, USA)

DEBORAH DIVITO -DIGREGORIO

*"The above picture is from the **'This House Is Not For Sale'** show in New York in 2018!!!*
He always puts on a great show. It used to be Aerosmith until my 1st Bon Jovi concert- He blows Aerosmith away when putting on a show!!"
Deborah DiVito-DiGregorio (North Babylon, New York, USA)

"I've been a fan since I was 14."
Lea Leiby (Pennsylvania, USA)

"I have been a HUGE fan the entire 35 years, I was a junior in high school then, we have been to so many of the concerts but it is never enough.
Their music has had such an impact on my life. Our daughters are being raised with the proper music education, all classic hard rock through my husband, who has a huge vinyl collection. We are taking them to see QUEEN in August.
The husband has claimed my original Bon Jovi vinyl, (it is MINE he cannot have it), we went last May to Milwaukee, for the final show at the Bradley Center, it was simply amazing, I begged him on social media to please sing 'AMEN' at the show, it is hands down my favorite song, so when Jon came into the crowd, just 2 sections away from me, I could not stop crying like I was 17 all over again. My husband was laughing at me but I knew he was thrilled that I finally got that close to Jon while he sang 'AMEN'. Always and forever a JOVI GIRL!!!"
DeAnne Lynnette (USA)

"I have been a fan of Bon Jovi since the beginning, sitting on the school bus in my high school years back in 1984 as a freshman begging our bus driver to tune into our local radio station so we could listen to our favorite rock songs.

My love of Bon Jovi continued through my teen years celebrating many milestones including graduation to 'Never Say Goodbye'.

Through the next stage of my life I followed Bon Jovi through their many albums. Fast forward to married life, work and children and a sudden loss to my family. During all of the above I still continued my love of the band, carried on being a member of 'BSWJBJ', making new friends from all over the country and world for that matter!

After the sudden loss of a family member I decided that you only live once and that although I had many responsibilities to attend to with marriage, work and children I decided to start touring and taking time for myself a bit again.

With the loving support of my husband and the 'honor' system of a wonderful fan from Norway we decided to meet for a private fan club show that would finally introduce me to the best bunch of fans that have become lifelong friends! That particular, show my husband drove me there in a snowstorm to meet up with a bunch of 'strangers' I met on the 'BSWJBJ' chat room! From that chat room one of the girls set up a private group for us to keep in touch. We all planned it and decided to make the trek to Sayreville to see the band! It was a meeting that is one of the best decisions I have ever made, if not for that trip I would have never met and become friends with these women. They came from Singapore, Sweden, UK, Virginia, New York, Germany, Canada and every single one of them piled into my car and my wonderful husband drove us to the show!

It was a meeting of the world!

Our love of touring continues to many places not always the entire group but we still share our experiences together and try to get together whenever the opportunity arises.

If it weren't for this band I wouldn't have met especially two of the most wonderful women, one from NY and one from FL that I'm honored to call my friends and travel buddies. We not only share a love for the band but many other things and now visit with each other outside of Bon Jovi shows as well.

I have been able to show my children that if you work hard you can reward yourself with things you love it isn't about money - it's about life and experiences. It has given me the balance in my life and best of all I have 100% support from my husband.

What more could a girl ask for!?"

Stacey Arakelian Towle (Sutton nr. Boston, Massachusetts, USA)

*"When I was captured in one of VH1 videos at Giant Stadium to '**Wanted Dead or Alive**' with all my great friends I met through 'Backstage Bon Jovi Fan Club' so many more memories."*
Michele Penna (New York)

"The Fast Lanes in Asbury Park, N.J.
This was back in 1993.
A very small place, so everyone was close to the band. I have seen Bon Jovi more then 40 times, but this time was the best."
Eileen Virgin-Neill (Moonachie, New Jersey)

*"When they did '**the Circle**' Tour. They played at Kansas Civic Center and it was on my Birthday. It was the best Birthday ever."*
Caryn Hurd (Camdenton, Missouri, USA)

"Bristol 2011 - my first VIP experience.
*I sang an awful rendition of '**It's My Life**' when no one else would pick up the mic, but I walked away with Tico's drum skin he had used in Oslo. Met David Bergmann and then the Diamond Circle.*
*Jon clapped eyes on me and pointed me out when singing chorus from '**Born To Be My Baby**'. I will never forget the whites of his eyes and his massive smile in that moment."*
Emma Ashcroft (Jacksonville, Florida, USA)

"2003, in Philly, Goo Goo Dolls opened.
I was 6 months pregnant, floor seating.
My husband and I spent like $300 per ticket, it was def worth it. When I stood up I could see the whole stage without moving.
When he took off his jacket I could see his superman tattoo."
Michelle Newton (Penn Yan, New York, USA)

"Pittsburgh, 2001.
*Ran my fingers through Jon's hair during '**Bed of Roses**'."*
Afsha Bee (Canada)

"Giants Stadium, Aug 8, 2003.
Probably the best set-list I've witnessed. Last show of the tour, and they opened with 'Twist & Shout'. Played 26 songs in total.
Great weather as well."
Brett Hutchison (Hillsdale, New Jersey, USA)

"Park West, Park City , Utah 1993."
Marcella Meadors (Salt Lake City, Utah)

"Those were the days."
Dorinda Lidstrom (Bremerton, Washington)

"Utica, NY was a good gig... 1987"
D. Farr (USA)

"Phillips Arena, April 20, 2018.
Went with all my girlfriends and Jon came to our section to do **'Bed of Roses'** *and* **'Amen'***.*
I've seen them 7 times, but that one will always be the best."
Allison Jones Zirbes (Chatsworth, Georgia)

"All of them."
Wendy Mitchell (Goldsboro, North Carolina)

"The last show for **'Slippery When Wet'** *tour in Hawaii that he had for his fan club.*
I was 17 and my mom got me the tickets to go best day of my life."
Nicole Brugh (Buchanan, Michigan)

*"***Slippery When Wet'** *in Milwaukee.*
Part of that footage is in the video for **'Raise your Hands'***."*
Joey Chudzinski (USA)

*"***This House is Not For Sale'** *Tour March, 2018 Houston, Texas.*
My seat was at the very top of The Toyota Center and it was the best concert I've been to in over 30yrs!
I went by myself cuz my hubby is more of a country music fan and besides my ticket was a little on the expensive side and he wasn't so happy about that! However, my hubby got over it and drove me downtown to the concert, paid to park, walked around bought me a $60.00 Bon Jovi shirt and waited until I got into the building.
While walking around the Toyota Center we seen a corner parking lot Reserved & roped off full of shiny, bright red RV buses. They weren't marked but had to be part of Bon Jovi's team. After I went into the concert my honey walked around and went to check out the 'House of Blues' to have a few beers. I told him the concert should be over around 10:30pm and I was close, it was about 10:45pm when Bon Jovi finished the last song."
Regina Duren (Humble, Texas)

"March 11 2011 MSG stands out for sure."
Irene Kirwan (Paterson, New Jersey)

*"**New Jersey**' tour with the catwalk all the way around the stadium.*
I could almost touch Jon.
Hardest working band in the business. Great show!!"
Lynnette Staley (Carmi, Illinois)

"Every Bon Jovi concert that I have been to since day 1 was totally amazing.
I will always love Bon Jovi."
Sandy Swafford (Fort Lauderdale, Florida)

*"July 26, 2003 '**Bed of Roses**' dance Philly, PA Veterans Stadium."*
Michelle Bloom (USA)

"Mohegan Sun...liplock."
Gloria McDermott (Meriden, Connecticut)

"Stuttgart in 1996. Aaaamazing."
Nina Stevenson (USA)

Atlanta 2011!!
Won tickets on the radio and 2018 had very, very good seats!
Jon sang 4 seats over from me!!!"
Cheryl Dennewitz Lanuza (Atlanta, Georgia)

"As far as concerts go, Bon Jovi is #1 (under Elvis), Neil Diamond is now #2. Don't miss either show!!!"
Victoria Alonge Guy (Harbor City, California)

"I just wanted you to now, from Dec 2017 thru Oct 2018, I was going thru a hard time in my life. It was Jon Bon Jovi's music and reading all about him on Facebook that got me thru that rough time in my life, and I am forever grateful for him and his music."
Mary Zilg Reinhard (New Bedford, Massachusetts)

"The two shows that happened to be on my birthday - May 5, 2001 (Cleveland) and May 5, 2018 (Mohegan Sun)."
Donna Sgroi (City Of Lauderdale Lakes, Florida)

"I wasn't allowed to listen to the current or popular music growing up. Small town life and it was the 3 C's.
'Country, Classical and Christian.'
In 1989, I got my first taste of Bon Jovi and fell in love.
By 1990, I moved to Ohio and had more access to current music and more radio stations. I did two decades worth of catching up in about two years.
Since then I have had every CD, most three times now (lost two collections).
Two concerts... two best ever!
Had a bidding war online to get an autographed CD.
Hands down, JBJ is THE best hair band, '80s band EVER.
He he.... he's my marriage freebie."
Kelly Moore (Huber Heights, Ohio)

"I've seen Bon Jovi about 15 times; all in NY & NJ.
*I've been a fan (for most of my Life) since I heard '**Runaway**' on the radio when I was around 15 yrs old.*
*I heard '**Runaway**' and immediately walked up to the record store to buy my very 1st Bon Jovi Album on Vinyl (which I still have and think I wore the album out!).*
Every concert I've been to has been great! Just being in an arena with Jon and the band, Jon singing and their music blasting, beating thru my body... It's the greatest feeling!
*However, the best one will be the one where I finally get to sit down in front of the stage. I haven't gotten there yet, but... '**Someday I'll Be Saturday Night**'!"*
Patricia Battaglia (USA)

*"February of 1989 Bon Jovi the '**New Jersey**' Tour!*
First off they were a lil wiser to the music business by that tour. Skid Row
opened up and I had front row seat and got called up on stage by Jon.
My heart sank... got to dance, sing and a hug and a kiss from him!
I also went and seen them a few other times and got pictures of the guys...
All of them are very down to earth!!"
Leslie D.Valle (USA)

"Jon shaking my hand and grabbed my poster, to sign...love that man
ever since... Down to earth as can be!
Leslie D.Valle (USA)

"Seen them 86 times!

My favorite show was at the Point Stadium in Johnstown PA – 'New Jersey' tour they had just sold out two nights in Pittsburgh at the civic arena and then came to little old Johnstown.

It was an outdoor show, poured down with rain and was far from sold out probably the only show on the whole tour not sold out.

Set list was different than other shows in the tour because of a random stage not the usual stage used very unique show for the tour and loved every min of it; best time of my life.

Also that night Bach from Skid Row was arrested for punching a police officer, the officer thought he had an alcoholic beverage which wasn't allowed there and he had water in a bottle. Fun times indeed."

Dana Cooper (Martinsburg, West Virginia)

Point Stadium, Johnstown, PA, 'New Jersey Syndicate' Tour, 16th June 1989

Have You Ever Seen the Rain?
Lay Your Hands on Me
I'd Die for You
Wild in the Streets
You Give Love a Bad Name
Tokyo Road
Born to Be My Baby
Let It Rock
I'll Be There For You
Blood on Blood
Runaway
Livin' on a Prayer
Ride Cowboy Ride
Wanted Dead or Alive
Bad Medicine

"May 1989 '__New Jersey__' tour, Charleston WV.
Attended with my best friend and her dad. It was fabulous.
They rocked it out for hours and didn't disappoint!
April 2018 Charlotte NC '__This House Is Not for Sale__' tour.
Attended this concert with my husband. He bought me tickets as my Valentine's Day gift because he knows how much I love them and have been a die-hard fan since '__Runaway__'.
We spent the weekend and the band did not disappoint in the least and Ritchie's replacements were OUTSTANDING!"
Christine Brewster (Bluefield, Virginia)

I loved all Bon Jovi concerts.
They were all great shows, '__The Circle__', '__Have a Nice Day__', '__This House Is Not for Sale__', etc. He always puts on the best shows.
Not many people can sound like they do on the radio but Bon Jovi does!"
Deborah DiVito-DiGregorio (North Babylon, New York)

"Loved them all."
Beverly Sorensen (Aroma Park, Illinois)

"In 2007 when they started with the '__Lost Highway__' tour I was so excited and my husband told me that if they came anywhere near us to get some tickets.
A few weeks later while at work he pulls up a confirmation email about Bon Jovi tickets and is unaware of where the Prudential Center is (we live on the Florida Georgia line). He Googled and sees that it's in New Jersey. I tell him that New Jersey is close. It's on the East Coast. It was an amazing concert."
Jennifer W. Brinkley (USA)

"Since 1984 I have loved Bon Jovi and every person that knows me or friends with me in Facebook knows this is my favorite band and anyways has and will be!
I have been to every concert that was close to me that I could afford to go to and the show never disappoints. I have always dreamed of meeting them they are so awesome!
'__Wanted Dead or Alive__' is my favorite.
I had a license plate made for the front of my car in the '80s that said 'Bon Jovi rocks your ass off' wish I still had it!
And I camped out in the snow for concert tickets for a concert once lol!"
Jamie Irene (USA)

"All my older brothers were there too (Donington, UK), I tried to hide under a bean bag in their transit van so I could go too: D
Still got the recording on tape."
Emma Ashcroft (Jacksonville, Florida, USA)

"Been a fan since 1983 and met him in person more than once! Nuff said."
Locaa Valle (USA)

"OMG I love, love Jon Bon Jovi.
Since I was a teen, I listened to his music - walking to High School - on my Walkman lol.
I absolutely love each and every one of his songs. OMG I have so many favorites can't pick just one. Jon's songs have gotten me thru so much as a teen and beyond. He is a blessing in disguise and it shows in all he does.
My sis took me to my first concert in Jersey – 'Because We Can' tour.
Then again I went with my friends in Jersey – 'What About Now' tour.
I badly want to see him again."
Lisa Greco Miguel (USA)

"I have been listening to Bon Jovi since the '80s.
My best friend Jamie got me listening to Bon Jovi when I was a teenager.
Bon Jovi is the No#1 Best Rock Band in the world.
I listen to Bon Jovi all the time."
Joy Caughorn (Knoxville, Tennessee, USA)

"I really wish Jon Bon Jovi would come back to Cincinnati to play again!!!"
Donna Futscher (Melbourne, Kentucky, USA)

"I love Bon Jovi because their music helped me through a difficult journey in my life.
Through each decision I had to make regarding surgery or treatment, their music, starting from 'Have A Nice Day' album to 'This House is Not for Sale' has lifted me up and pushed me forward to the next journey. Always wanted to meet Jon so I could tell him what he did for me in my life with the lyrics and music.
I am now cancer free and will be forever grateful to Bon Jovi for saving my life."
Lisa P. Burg (Davie, Florida, USA)

"Love all of their albums, I don't really have a favorite.
My first record I bought was 'Runaway'!
Pamela Chapman-Stivison (Kelso, Washington, USA)

"This one!!!"
Wendy Sue (USA)

"Because I caught this!!! #myfirstbonjoviconcert #fanforlife."
Wendy Sue (USA)

*"2003 '**Bounce**' Tour. SLC, UT.*
1st Bon Jovi concert ever.
I was 8 months prego. Had awesome seats by the catwalk off to the side.
I'm dying as he starts making his way down my way, as all the girls start to pile up to touch his hand as he reaches down.
I knew if I attempted to get any closer, my baby would get smashed, lol, so I just stood there frozen and snapped a pic instead.
Needless to say, I blinded him with my flash. I felt guilty that I had caused him to squint, but I couldn't help but feel a lil special too...
#BestConcertEver."
Melissa A. Jaynes (Salem, Utah)

"Yummy."
Kristen Saffian (USA)

"I've been to 24 concerts, best one New England where Kid Rock opened.
Took my wife to Dublin Ireland and went both nights."
Robert Uhrich (USA)

"March 2010. Probably the last time I will ever see them.
*It was '**the Circle**' tour and we went all in for VIP tickets and got seats on the floor...15 or so feet from '**the Circle**' part of the stage.*
I was about 15 feet from Jon.
In October of that year I got pregnant with my son. I knew that we were going to try for a baby, so I also knew it would probably be the last time I saw them in concert. It was also not long after that, that Richie left the band."
Lisa Howard Glass (USA)

"I've been a super huge fan of Bon Jovi since the beginning of 1983, they have always put on the best shows I've ever had the privilege of seeing. From flying in the air, popping out of the floor, to running on a bridge to get to the fans that are so far away - it was awesome.
One show that scared me was a show they did in Arizona where Jon was touching the fans hands when all of the sudden he was yanked into the crowd it seemed like forever for security to find him and finally they did and you could see that he was not happy, but true to form he handled it like a true gentleman with a heart of gold and finished the show!!!!!
Bon Jovi Forever..."
Tiffany Hatt (Ranchitos Verde, Arizona, USA)

"I have been a Bon Jovi fan since the beginning in 1983. My dad got sick. He started having really bad heart pains and shortness of breath. I listened to Bon Jovi to help get me through. I was the only black girl listening to them and everyone else was into Michael Jackson and Prince. I like and respected them, but they are no Bon Jovi.

*I finally wore them down, you get the captain of the football team and his buddies singing '**Livin' On A Prayer**', you're doing something right.*

My dad had 2 heart attacks and the dr. said he couldn't have surgery. While in the hospital he had another heart attack.

I felt so helpless and alone. My mom was so busy with the dr., my sister was with her boyfriend and I was alone.

I kept listening to Bon Jovi and their music got me through.

My dad finally recovered. I wrote a letter to them and in those days Jon's mom was the head of the fan club. I told them my story and she made me in charge of the mid-west branch of the fan club for a couple of years and I met the guys. Richie even sent me a picture with him kissing baby Ava and Heather when she was born.

I also know the know the band 7th Heaven who opened for Bon Jovi. They are really nice guys. The lead singer has changed since I first met them. They are really great and nice guys.

I tried for years to get Bon Jovi into Hall of Fame. A few years ago I asked them what needed to be done and why was it taking so long.

I gathered all my friends and told them to vote to get the fan vote.

Once they get the vote we had to do it again. When they won and got over 1 million votes I was ecstatic.

You thought I won. Everyone congratulated me, it was so funny.

I am so happy and proud of them. It was a long time coming. They mean do much to me. I love them so much. Bon Jovi is the best band in the world. As long as they play 'I'll Be There For Them'."
Angela Love (Chicago, Illinois)

"All 19 of their shows."
Barbara Wise (Dunnellon, Florida)

"Ft. Lauderdale Fla 2017."
Debbie Fine (Fort Lauderdale, Florida)

"I have been listening to Bon Jovi since the '80s and still no#1 rock band in the world...
I listen to Bon Jovi constantly... Bon Jovi is the best...
I'm Bon Jovi no#1 fan and I always will be."
Joy Caughorn (Knoxville, Tennessee, USA)

*"2018 Denver rescheduled from 2017 '**THNFS**'.*
He said he would make it up to us and was a man of his word - why I'm a big fan.
Pre, pre-sale tickets at half price! Was in 6th row, once in a lifetime seats.
Had lost my husband of 25 years unexpectedly in between the dates and the concert in 2018 was my first real outing and definitely first time smiling since my husband passed.
Forever grateful.
Oh and we just 'happened' to get to the entrance door at the right time. The usher escorted us to our seating area around the backstage hallways. We got to see and touch the cases that held their equipment.
Higher power at work there.
I could feel my husband's presence with me."
Becky Hersey (Parker, Colorado)

"1984 in New Jersey."
Paul Pisano (USA)

"My Mother's day gift.
The concert was in Atlanta on May the 11 2001.
We were standing in our seats and Richie spotted us and then John came over and he spotted us and it was just like the best thing ever other than the birth of my children and I will never forget that.
I love you so much JBJ you are the greatest ever."
Hope Green (Carrollton, GA, USA)

"I love everything about Bon Jovi, I have been a huge fan since they first came out.
*I fought Cancer for 8 yrs on and off and let me tell you I was so ready to give up plenty of times, but my husband and my kids and Bon Jovi's music got me thru it all mostly '**Keep the Faith**' and '**Livin' On a Prayer**' and the sound of Jon's voice when he sang those songs made me want to fight even harder.*
Even at the worst times where I didn't think I could go on but every time I heard those songs it pulled me thru every time.
Thank you Bon Jovi for all you did and do and still continue to do."
Debbie Calabrese Masko (Blakely, Pennsylvania, USA)

"I am a die hard 72, now he is keeping my heritage alive with honor and grace."
Emily Katau King (USA)

*"The Greenville, SC show for the '**Have a Nice Day**' tour was memorable to me for a few reasons.*

First, it was added after the original listing, and it was close to my home, so I was super excited.

Next, this show was special because it gave me a 'hand touch' with Mr. Jon himself.

Third, JBJ had something to prove, and he sure did just that!

This show was only six days after Heather left Richie, so it seemed they were being super supportive of Sambora, and wow they did a great show. Such a sad time for Richie, but a somewhat angry Jon with something to prove gives some energy to the performances.

Bristow, VA show in July 2003 was a fabulous show because it was half acoustic and half electric.

*It was the first and only time I've heard '**Something to Believe In**' live. Extreme heat but so worth it!"*

Melissa Martin Collins (USA)

"Went to a concert back in the '80s my first.

It was so Awesome!

My boyfriend now husband surprised me. Could be the reason.

Hahaha. I so love this band!

Didn't tell my mom I was going because she didn't want me going to concerts. I was hoarse the next morning from yelling and she asked why. I told her - she wasn't happy, but my dad laughed."

Kelley Ladwig (Gilbert, Louisiana, USA)

"Too many things, I could tell... nuff said!"

Leslie D. Valle **(USA)**

"Giants stadium, 1989."

June Sarazen (USA)

"I first heard of Bon Jovi when I was 14 years old and I'm 51 now. Always gets better.

Every concert I have seen is always top notch.

Still listen to his music everyday. His music gives me the positive attitude I need to start my day. Much Love!!!"

Angela Wyatt Justice (USA)

"So many memories..."

Linda Abitz (USA)

"I grew up with John in Sayreville.
Worked and help out way before and into the Band itself. I had worked,
helped and was friends in circles we hung out in.
The one thing that did keep us together was John's playing days whether
it was a downstairs 16th birthday party or a block dance, he played at I
was around up until around '90-'91.
I saved the whole bands ass when our rental truck wouldn't start at 3am,
which was closing time in those days.
When John recorded Runaway from his detail riding a bus from a bus
stop on Rte. 9 north in a gas station that is now destroyed but he when he
got the job at the Power Station he didn't even have a car so the first
couple months he had take the bus to the NY Port Authority bus station
on 42 and 7th.
The Power Station was on 53 and 9th so he needed to walk there at first.
So when he did he had to walk by the characters, all the people there.
Up until then all John's songs were just love songs and such not very
good, so a friend of John's and basically his first manager knew a guy
who was a master songwriter named George Karakolou and he told John
that he should maybe see if they could write some songs.
*In that day 2 songs were written unreleased '**Hollywood Dreams**' and*
*'**Runaway**'.*

GARY GEORGE

So when his cousin Tony Bongiovi gave him the job to sweep floors and just do odd jobs and gofer - the real thing that came out of that was free recording time. So when John used to make those walks he would notice all girl and prostitutes there so that's what the details of '**Runaway**' are about.

When he gave that demo to the Radio Station APP and when he started to play on the radio they put on the album from local talent so that's when it really started to go to other major cities in the US and he ended winning that but what the problem was he didn't have a band and the only one he was keeping was David so what he had to do was get a band.

So he had to put one together. I know you probably know how the band was formed but one last key position was needed 'lead guitarist'.

So I used to go to this Bar called 'Charlie's Uncle' on Rte. 18 north in East Brunswick NJ and he used to have a band Message Board. But also every Wed Richie Sambora and friends played there and I knew 2 girls who were his friends, so I knew Richie also because he would with sit us between sets.

When Richie found out that John was searching around for a guitar player we were down at the Fountain Casino and John was playing it wasn't even Bon Jovi but Richie ended up coming down to watch and I was with a friend that used to work in Princeton, NJ at the Macarthur Theatre and they really needed some who knew how to set up things.

One night I was helping out and Richie came down to watch. I was sitting on the stage always, so after it was over Richie comes up and says to John "I am going to be your lead guitarist"

and he hi-fived him, so it ended up that he was in then band.

They had him come over to Pete's basement to see what he could do, he was then 'in' so the band is together and they signed the contract the album got recorded and '**Runaway**' is a hit!!

So Bon Jovi is a band, the album is recorded and they were waiting for the release date and Terry is still helping out and they had a gig at the Fountain Casino behind Scandal the top band. They were renting those little moving trucks to move things, now it was March 1983 but I can't remember the exact date but it was 3 months before the album came out. I was still around and it was crazy that I did know them both and they knew me. That was karma or something.

So Terry and Pete were still the 2 people helping out and I came down to just help out.

It is then official Bon Jovi (actually PolyGram) wants to call it 'Intruder', so they all get together at John's mother's 'Mrs B'. so

They are trying to get a name for the band - I wasn't Terry was though - so they are all thinking and John says how about Bon Jovi and everybody *started laughing it sound like a spaghetti sauce, but it ends up as Bon Jovi.*

His name is Terry McNamara so Terry and Peter Mantas who was John's best friend since about 7 years old and Pete also knew Terry because he was dating his sister Maura unfortunately she ended up dying way later at my house from just bad health.

Terry was living with me after my divorce. I only took her in because she had nowhere else to stay. I just did it out of just kindness she couldn't even pay me so what happened was Terry ended working helping Pete put and move all the equipment together and at that time they were playing every Sunday at the Fastlane in Asbury Park NJ when it was 'John Bongiovi and the Wild Ones'. I used to help out sometimes just to get in for free and help them set up. They were only getting paid $150 a night so Terry would many get $15 dollars how do split that with the band 5 and 2 helpers so I just did for the music and just to help them out since I was friends with all of them, I never got any money.

So as this goes along 'the Wild Ones' lasted one summer it was 1981 or '82. Right after that John had no band but he would sing around town in a band Pete would was in called 'Two Fold' that was just something he did because he was trying to get another band together, but Terry was always there.

I would help out sometimes, I had a van and sometimes I just helped out so eventually everything comes together.

So it is. 3 months before the release date so they had gig backing up the band Scandal and Bon Jovi was back up and it was at the Fountain Casino again and they were renting moving trucks now for gigs now so I came down to see it and Terry and Pete were set up guys and I didn't make it down to help set up but I was there in the upstairs dressing room it as the first time I saw both of them together and Richie see me and says - "What are doing here?"

He didn't know I knew John and it was really crazy that I knew both of them John good, Richie just knew who I was and I don't think it was Karma that happened so everything went well.

I was on the stage with Terry just hanging out and the night is over and they are ready to start loading up - it is 3 Am in morning - Terry asked me to get the truck and I go out and it isn't starting up, nope 'broke down'. So everybody is saying 'what r we going to do?' and I just said
"I can use my van we just need to keep going, to make a lot of trips"
and John asked me if I wanted money and I wasn't going to take any money I told him when the album comes sign it, I will come by your house and pick it up.

So it ends up that it took 3 of us till 7am to move the gear from Matawan to the Rehearsal studio in a closed down Woodbridge Health club that is about 1 hour to drive and load and unload $70,000 thousand dollars of equipment and the piano is like 100 pounds so John is happy and it finally is all done at 8am.

Then they go out on a little 3 month mini tour of colleges with Eddie Money, so I forget about the album.

I haven't seen John in couple months, but the album comes out and then one day I come home and my mother says somebody came by and dropped this off. John had gotten 10 'not for sale For Promotional use only' albums. John had remembered, stopped by and dropped one off.

I was surprised because I didn't care I just did it to help out friends.

But what happened then was I was living at my girlfriends mothers house Kim Deatherage on Johnson lane in Sayreville and I had 200 albums and one night somebody broke in and stole all of them I had a lot rare stuff in that house and the album John gave had gone. It was somebody who knew it was there, probably somebody I thought was a friend.

So I am the only person to move all the equipment for the band Bon Jovi that is good thing to know but only a few people know about it when they were inducted I felt that I was included in John's speech.

I knew John well back in those days and I know a lot of other stuff - stories about John and all of the band in the early years. I was a good friend of John's mother, for some reason she liked me more than a lot of people.

I used to be in John's house a lot because she liked me. I was always welcome there and no matter she always let me in the house even if John wasn't home. She would drink wine with me and she wanted to teach me how to play bridge and she wanted me to fill in, but I didn't - that would have been good idea to play with Mrs B at Bridge club.

I was 2 years ahead of John in high school. He only went to Sayreville High for 11 and 12 grade before Pete and John went to all male catholic school in South Amboy. But they convinced their parents to let them go to Sayreville.

John had a hard time in high school for some reason I don't know why the guys I guess didn't like him I had no problem John was a shy person he wasn't like that until after the music, when he changed. We brought him to Terry's house one day and Terry says

"You see this guy, he will be famous sometime."

And he just went red, it was weird his reaction to me.
I don't have a single autograph left I will never ask him but I got so much stuff for many.

GARY GEORGE

I might see him the next time he touts around here in Jersey. But the whole band is from Jersey and the list is long most of the time I have to go out of state to get passes.
The fan club is the first printing Mrs B. made. If you look at you can see she wrote 'if you need tickets stop by Mrs B' that is her handwriting. Back stage with a Bon Jovi by mail I helped her out she gave me a lot of them and I went around and gave people them that is last original copy the other is when I joined probably one of the first couple of people to join $15 dollars to join.
I used to see her at the club, which was in a building in the basement where the Flower shop was and his Father's salon, but nobody knew because it was post office box.
I used to get all my tickets there until it moved and I never found out were it went. I stopped by one day and his father was there he didn't know me well he was never home. I never saw his father home and I passed there almost everyday it was the shortest route from Hillside Ave (my home) to Johnson's lane. I used to see John because of that.
I can tell you John when he was 12 or 13 used to walk from Robin Hood Dr. to Johnson Lane and knock on Kim's door and said
"Is Kimme home?" He had crush on my girlfriend when he was 12 or 13. That is why I first met him because she was a very pretty, good looking girl, so on day she tells me to go there with her that was the first time I met him. Kim's mother told me that I never did but when I did I went and

told him about and he got so embarrassed it was just busting his balls, but he didn't think it was funny though.

"When Richie Sambora joined the band, he had a 'Personal Management Contract'. I think his name was Ed; Doc McGhee bought it out from Ed. The reason I mention this is because Ed was a partner in a club In Sayreville, 'Modern Times' now the 'Starland Ballroom'. When we were growing up it was called 'Willy's'.

John got permission from Ed to rehearse there; this was 'Pre-Doc' by a few months.

Bon Jovi got to rehearse 2 Days a week in the Backroom, there was a stage in there as it was at that time 2 rooms. Front was a Bar; back was sort of a club. I mention this because there was always a band there on the same days when they rehearsed waiting for Bon Jovi to finish.

They were heavy metal looking bunch.

Growing up in Sayreville. I would watch them for a bit after Bon Jovi were done a few times and they were playing hard rock.

Turns out it was Metallica! James, Cliff Burton, Dave Mustaine and Lars Ulrich.

Johnny Z of 'Megaforce' - which was a small label at the time - he owned this small record store in New Brunswick, NJ, I used to go there to buy vinyl. He had moved them to Old Bridge, they had a bunch of kids there they called the Metal Militia. They had this East Brunswick flea market had to be 1982. It is really hard to remember the years now.

I saw the Metallica play - there must have only been 50 people there - so it ends up that Metallica was rehearsing after Bon Jovi at the same place. RIP Cliff Burton. Lars was cool, too.

Years later one time I ran into James Hetfield at a show and said hello and asked him if he remembered rehearsing in Sayreville? He said yes, and then I said do you know who that band was before you guys? He had no idea, I told him it was Bon Jovi and he said are you kidding me! So it ends up Bon Jovi and Metallica we're both rehearsing at I think it was 'Modern Times' - it changed names so many times.

Just a cool story how 2 powerhouse rock bands rehearsed right after each other in a club in Sayreville where Skid Row would play, also Dave Sabo at first was almost John's lead guitar player, but he was 2 years younger and just wasn't good enough then. But they did make huge fame in the early '90s.

If you want to hear about the front album cover shoot John had a bad time at that shoot .Doc was the manager and needed to get an Album cover shot.

The band met at Doc's office above Mickey Mantles near Columbus Circle.

The photographer for the 1st time was Geoffrey I forget who his last name is.

'The Girl' was getting her makeup done - it was wintertime.

The plan was, John walked across from Doc's office a block or two and set up the shot. The band away from John, when the light down the block would turn Red, onto the street he would go and take some shots.

If you look closely at Jon with his cut off leather jacket he was freezing. He was pissed at Pete the whole time because his job was to stop people from crossing the street behind the shot. Pete was the only person trying to yell at people not to cross. John was giving Pete dirty looks, cause he was cold.

Pete was behind that white car, keeping people from crossing the street. John told me about the whole thing. John is telling Pete 'don't let people cross the street'.

Needless to say they got it done.

I got into trouble a few times with John getting pissed at me; they were at the same place doing retakes for one video.

I was on the stage and somebody gives me a 35mm camera to take some pics. I was trying not to fall off the stage while taking pictures. I ended up getting to close John and he shuts down the whole shoot - must have been 1000 people there.

He got pissed at me and over the mic says "Gary you can't be there."

I was so embarrassed. I saw John a few days later and told him I just wasn't paying attention trying to get pics. He just said everybody just wanted to go home. I shouldn't have said that to you. John could get pissed really easy sometimes. But he never held it against you."

Gary George (Sayreville, New Jersey)

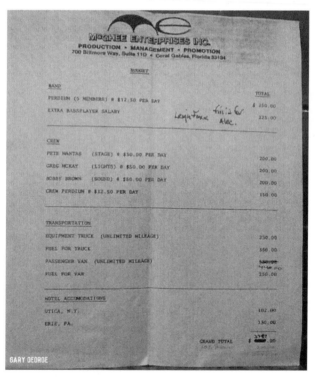

*"My favorite, 'best' concert was Bon Jovi's '**Slippery When Wet**' at Giant Stadium on New Years Eve.*
My friend Peter got me hooked and I've been a fan ever since.
Even better I got front row at his second Christmas show at the Count Basie Theater in Red Bank in '91.
They are so Great and Awesome in concert. I'm very proud to be their fan for 34 year's."
Tina Stano (Keansburg, New Jersey)

"I've followed the band Bon Jovi for over 35 years, seen all the videos I could - will always luv Bon Jovi."
Brenda Headley (Coshocton, Ohio)

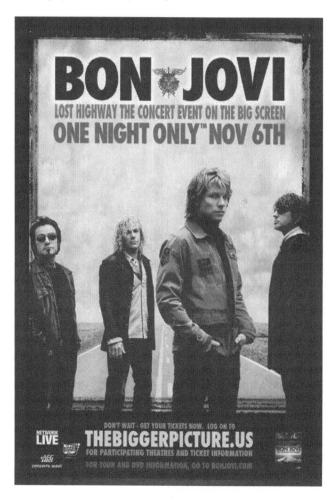

This House Is Not for Sale – Live from the London Palladium

1) This House Is Not for Sale.......6:36
2) Living With the Ghost...........5:05
3) Knockout........................3:38
4) Labor of Love...................5:51
5) Born Again Tomorrow.........4:07
6) Roller Coaster...................3:44
7) New Year's Day.................4:32
8) The Devil's in the Temple......3:22
9) Scars on This Guitar...........5:31
10) God Bless This Mess............3:18
11) Reunion........................4:15
12) Real Love......................4:43
13) All Hail the King.................6:08
14) We Don't Run...................4:01
15) Come On Up to Our House......5:38

Release Date: 16ᵗʰ December 2016
Producer: Obie O'Brien
Singles: None

"Love this album. I have no problem with the different style it suits his voice of today."
Donna Watson (Wales, UK)

"I was at the London Palladium, I had won tickets.
It was an amazing show, first time I had been at a record debut Jon and the rest of the guys was on fire it was good to hear the story behind the songs hope to go to another."
Madeline Steer (Habrough, UK)

"Looks hottttt!"
June Sarazen (In the World)

"You rock Jon."
Yvonne Young (Cumbernauld, Scotland, UK)

"My love."
Sabina Gaskin (Lutjbroek, Netherlands)

"I'm happy that these people are still so creative and full of energy."
Olga Adamczyk (In the World)

199

"Ur my rock 'n' roll hero Jon."
Brenda Headley (Coshocton, Ohio)

"He said this was his 'I'm a pissed off album - I had a lot to say'.
I therefore love him being pissed off.
*My favourite 2 songs (as I can't choose between them) are **'Living With**
The Ghost' and **'Scars on This Guitar'**.*
Never played them at my last concert at Anfield, but they can't play them
all!
Once a Jovi girl, always a Jovi girl."
Donna Brimson (Portsmouth, UK)

"I saw the concerts in Bucharest.
I really like his music.
Since the '80s I am a hard-core fan. I respect him for his charitable
actions.
*I don't get tired of listening to **'Bed of Roses'**."*
Doina Carmen (Constanta, Romania)

Bon Jovi 'the Albums' UK & USA Chart Success

Title	Year	UK	USA
Bon Jovi	1984	71	43
7800 Fahrenheit	1985	28	37
Slippery When Wet	1986	1	6
New Jersey	1988	1	1
Keep the faith	1992	1	5
Cross Road	1994	1	8
These Days	1995	1	9
Crush	2000	1	9
One Wild Night Live	2001	2	20
Bounce	2002	2	2
This Left Feels Right	2003	4	14
100,000,000 Bon Jovi Fans Can't Be Wrong	2004	90	53
Have a Nice Day	2005	2	2
Lost Highway	2007	2	1
The Circle	2009	2	1
Greatest Hits	2010	2	5
Inside Out	2012	-	196
What About Now	2013	2	1
Burning Bridges	2015	3	13
This House Is Not for Sale	2016	5	1
This House Is Not for Sale – Live at the London Palladium	2016	-	-

Bon Jovi 'the Singles' UK & USA Chart Success

Title	Year	UK	USA
Runaway	1984	"	39
She Don't Know Me	1984	"	48
Burning For Love	1984	"	"
Only Lonely	1985	"	54
In and Out of Love	1985	"	69
The Hardest Part is the Night	1985	68	"
Silent Night	1985	"	"
You Give Love a Bad Name	1986	14	1
Livin' on a Prayer	1986	4	1
Wanted Dead or Alive	1987	13	7
Never Say Goodbye	1987	21	"
Bad Medicine	1988	17	1
Born to Be My Baby	1988	22	3
I'll Be There for You	1989	18	1
Lay Your Hands on Me	1989	18	7
Living in Sin	1989	35	9
Keep the Faith	1992	5	29
Bed of Roses	1993	13	10
In These Arms	1993	9	27
I'll Sleep When I'm Dead	1993	17	97
I Believe	1993	11	"

Dry County	1994	9	"
Please Come Home for Christmas	1994	7	"
Always	1994	2	4
Someday I'll Be Saturday Night	1995	7	"
This Ain't a Love Song	1995	6	14
Something for the Pain	1995	8	76
Lie to Me	1995	10	88
These Days	1996	7	"
Hey God	1996	13	"
Real Life	1999	21	"
It's My Life	2000	3	33
Say It Isn't So	2000	10	"
Thank You for Loving Me	2000	12	57
One Wild Night (2001)	2001	10	"
Wanted Dead or Alive (Live)	2001	"	"
Everyday	2002	5	118
Bounce	2002	"	"
Misunderstood	2002	21	106
All About Lovin' You	2003	9	"
The Distance	2003	"	"
Wanted Dead or Alive (2003)	2003	"	"
It's My Life (2003)	2003	"	"
Have a Nice Day	2005	6	53
Who Says You Can't Go Home	2005	5	23

Welcome to Wherever You Are	2006	19	"
(You Want To) Make a Memory	2007	33	27
Lost Highway	2007	117	"
Till We Ain't Strangers Anymore	2007	"	123
Summertime	2007	"	"
Whole Lot of Leavin'	2008	"	"
We Weren't Born to Follow	2009	25	68
Superman Tonight	2010	"	"
When We Were Beautiful	2010	"	"
What Do You Got?	2010	127	102
No Apologies	2011	"	"
This Is Our House	2011	"	"
Because We Can	2013	38	106
What About Now	2013	"	"
We Don't Run	2015	"	"
Saturday Night Gave Me Sunday Morning	2015	"	"
This House Is Not for Sale	2016	130	"
Knockout	2016	"	"
Labor of Love	2016	"	"
Born Again Tomorrow	2016	"	"
When We Were Us	2018	"	"
Walls	2018	"	"

47943156R00116

Printed in Poland
by Amazon Fulfillment
Poland Sp. z o.o., Wrocław